THE RIDER'S HANDBOOK

THE RIDER'S HANDBOOK

Jeanne K. Posey

ARCO PUBLISHING COMPANY INC.

219 Park Avenue South, New York, N.Y. 10003

Published by Arco Publishing Company, Inc.
219 Park Avenue South, New York, N.Y. 10003

Library of Congress Cataloging in Publication Data

Posey, Jeanne K
  The rider's handbook.

  Includes index.
    1. Horsemanship.
I. Title.

SF309.P8   798'.23   75-15135
ISBN 0-668-03854-3

Printed in the United States of America

To Pat and Ron

Contents

THE RIDER'S HANDBOOK

Understanding Your Horse

Whether you own your own horse or ride someone else's (at a riding stable or a friend's) you will find it much easier to become a successful rider if you develop a relationship with the horse. Riding is communicating with the horse, getting him to do what you want him to do. You will enjoy riding much more if you establish a rapport with your horse and if he performs willingly and quickly, with a minimum of effort on your part and on his. It takes time and careful effort to develop this kind of relationship with a horse. Although it is much easier to achieve it with a horse that you care for yourself, you can also do it with one that you ride only occasionally and do not feed and care for between rides.

The first step toward establishing this rapport is to get the horse to like you and to associate good things with you. Once he has accepted you as a friend, you can strengthen the relationship by making your rides as pleasant as possible for the horse, while still expecting him to perform. Try to keep his rides comfortable and pleasant but at the same time don't let him get away with bad habits that are unpleasant or uncomfortable for you. Both horse and rider must be happy in order for riding to become really enjoyable.

One way to keep riding comfortable is to keep the work you ask the horse to perform within the scope of his physical ability. You should not overtax the horse or try to get him to do something that is too difficult for his age, condition, or stage of training. Don't expect a two-year-old to jump high jumps, for instance, or try to complete a 50- or 100-mile ride on a horse that has only been ridden once or twice a month.

In addition to developing a friendly relationship with your horse, you should try to learn as much as possible about horses and how they think. Reading books about horses and riding will help, and talking to knowledgeable riders and trainers will also give you some ideas. Most of the knowledge you gain, however, will probably come from observing horses and riders, and from riding and learning from your experiences. You will learn, for instance, which undesirable habits your horse seems most likely to develop. Some horses never seem to get over their desire to return to the barn or to join other horses, for example, while others never show any tendency to do this at all.

As you read books and talk to people, you will get all kinds of advice about how to ride and handle your horse. You will have to decide for yourself whether or not to take the advice. Because horses are individuals, it is important that you realize that there is no set way to ride or to handle a horse, although there are certain guidelines on form, how to give signals, etc., which are useful. These rules of riding are followed because they have been found to be the most effective for a majority of horses. A rider should always be ready to improvise, however, in case his horse does not respond to the method he is trying. Any method of riding or training that is logical and not dangerous is probably worth trying if the established methods do not work.

Keep in mind that horses, however smart they may seem, do not reason like humans. They learn by association and by forming habits, and they learn bad habits just as quickly as good ones. A horse repeats any action that is pleasant or that gets him out of work. Thus he is naturally inclined to head for the barn or other place where he gets to rest. He'll avoid any action that causes pain or discomfort, and if being ridden causes discomfort he will be quite ingenious at getting out of it.

Horses have certain characteristics that you should keep in mind. First, they are very timid for their size, and often react violently to seemingly trivial things. For instance, any sudden movement or noise behind a horse may cause him to bolt forward or to kick. Another thing to remember is that horses have a strong herd instinct. They prefer the company of their friends to your company at most times, and will be reluctant to leave other horses or the barn area. While horses can't talk, they will show you when they are tired, in pain, or generally unhappy. When a normally willing horse goes with his head down, his ears back, or becomes balky or listless, he probably doesn't feel well, or may have sore muscles. By the same token, a normally quiet, calm horse that becomes excitable and restless should be examined closely. Unusual behavior under saddle should be taken as a warning that something is wrong with the horse.

One of the things you should study if you plan to ride horses is their anatomy and how they move. You can do this by reading books and by observing horses at play, in the pasture, and while being ridden by other people. It will help both you and the horse if you understand how he moves when you are riding him.

If you watch horses while they are loose in the field, you will notice that they depend greatly on their heads and necks for balance as they run, stop, turn, and jump. When the weight of a rider is added, the horse must use his head and neck even more to adjust his balance to accommodate the rider, much as a person uses his hands and arms when carrying a load on his back or head. The rider should try to ride so that he interferes as little as possible with these balancing gestures. Constantly keeping the reins tight and pulling the horse's head out of position forces him to abandon his natural balancing aids and depend entirely on his back and legs. This not only puts more strain on these parts, but also limits his athletic ability. When a rider has been doing this to his horse for a long time, he may not realize how stiff and clumsy the horse has become. If he rides a friend's horse that has been ridden correctly, he may be surprised at how easily this horse performs movements which his horse cannot.

A rider who consistently sits off balance, or who rides in such a way that keeps the horse in a state of anxiety, also limits his horse's ability. If the horse has to work to keep himself on his feet, or worries about keeping a severe bit off his tender mouth, or is pressured about how fast he must work, he cannot possibly relax and become a pleasure to ride.

The rider should learn as much as possible about the horse's physical structure and balance so he can ride to help, not hinder, the horse's movements. A horse's muscular system is complex, but basically he is a "rear-engined" animal whose legs are drawn forward by the large muscles in the neck and back, and drawn back by the muscles in the upper legs, shoulders, and haunches. Poor riding habits can interfere with the horse's natural strides by causing him to shorten up to compensate for incorrect shifts in weight or poorly timed hand signals.

If a rider understands how the horse's legs move during the different gaits, he can more easily learn to control the horse's speed, direction, cadence, and gait. He can then learn to judge when to ask for a change of pace or when to change leads in a canter.

Horses generally have four gaits (three if you count the canter and gallop as one gait). The usual gaits are the walk, trot, canter, and gallop. A rider quickly learns to distinguish among the gaits while riding and while watching horses in the field, but it is not enough to be able to recognize the different gaits in action. The rider should learn how the legs move in each gait so that he can feel what the horse is doing.

The walk is the horse's most important gait, yet it is often neglected by the beginning rider. "Learn to walk before you run" is very meaningful in riding, since the horse cannot perform at faster gaits satisfactorily until he can work well and in control at a walk.

The walk is a "four beat lateral gait." "Four beat" means that the horse takes four steps in each stride. (A step is the movement of one foot or two feet in unison within a stride; a stride is the distance from when the first hoof strikes the ground to when the last of the four hooves strikes. In the walk each leg moves separately, the legs on each side moving in sequence; this is called lateral action.) If you listen to a horse walking on pavement you will hear four distinct sounds within each stride.

The trot is faster than a walk and is usually slower than a canter or gallop, although some horses can trot faster than they can run (for example, Standardbred harness horses). The trot is often the horse's favorite gait. It is the least tiring of the gaits for a long period of time, and many horses favor it to save energy. The trot is less tiring than the gallop or canter because it is a two-beat gait and there are always two feet supporting the horse. The trot is a two-beat diagonal gait, with the left front and right hind moving forward and striking together, and the right front and left hind. The left fore and right hind are called the "left diagonal" and vice-versa.

If the horse is favoring one diagonal (keeping weight off it by leaning to the other side), one of the two sounds of the trotting stride will be louder than the other. While the horse normally nods his head in the walk and canter, he should not do this in the trot. Nodding the head in the trot is a sign of lameness. Occasionally, however, a horse will characteristically move his head from side to side at a trot, which may be his own peculiar way of going, and not unsoundness.

When a rider "posts" to the trot, he rides on one diagonal. As the diagonal pair of legs moves forward, the rider rises in his stirrups, and as the legs strike the ground and support the horse's forward motion, the rider lets his weight return to the saddle. Since horses naturally favor one side or the other, the rider will be thrown to the horse's favorite diagonal when he begins to post, unless he consciously waits and picks up the diagonal of his choice. The horse works harder on whichever diagonal pair the rider uses. In a ring the rider should post to the "outside" diagonal (nearest the fence) so that the horse supports the rider's weight with the "inside" hind leg. This helps maintain the horse's balance as he travels in the circle, since he naturally leans a little toward the inside. Posting on the wrong diagonal on a circle may noticeably affect the smoothness of the horse's way of going. How much it affects the horse's balance will depend on the horse's general athletic ability and on the size of the rider in relation to the horse.

In pleasure riding it usually doesn't matter which diagonal the rider uses *as long as he doesn't post on the same one all of the time.* This will develop one set of muscles more fully than the other and will encourage the horse to be even more one-sided than he naturally is.

You can change your diagonal without changing gait or speed by sitting half of a stride (missing one rise) and posting again. This can best be explained as "sit one bump" and rise to the next stride. You can check your diagonal by watching the horse's shoulders as you rise to the trot: whichever shoulder you rise with is the diagonal you are on. Later you should be able to feel the diagonal as you relax and feel for the movement of the horse's back and legs under you.

As you probably have noticed, not all horses trot. Some have other intermediate gaits that fall between the walk and the canter. These are the "lateral gaits," which include the pace, amble, and running walk. Horses with Standardbred, Saddlebred, or Tennessee Walking Horse blood often have lateral gaits. Such horses are known, in general, as "gaited horses."

The ability to perform lateral gaits is apparently inherited, and may show up in odd places in cross-bred horses. A gaited horse may or may not have gaited offspring, depending on what kind of horse it is bred to. The ability to perform gaits other than the trot is caused by a difference in the nervous system. Because the gaited horse uses a different set of muscles than the trotter, gaited horses may have some difficulty in performing the canter, which uses both lateral and diagonal muscles. Some gaited horses may not canter at all, or rarely, while others may be able to do four or five different gaits. The rack, which is the high-stepping, flashy gait used in five-gaited American Saddlebred classes, is supposedly an artificial gait. Many people however, claim that their horses do it naturally. The rack can best be described as a four-beat trot at high speed, thus the term "single-foot."

Lovers of gaited horses claim their lateral gaits to be more comfortable than those of trotting horses. Personally, I find the lateral gaits to be unnatural feeling, but that may be because I was raised on trotting horses. The lateral gaits give a side-to-side motion to the rider, rather than an up-and-down motion as do the diagonal gaits.

When we talk about the canter, the word "leads" will undoubtedly pop into the heads of many horse owners and/or riders. Anyone who has ever been to a horse show knows how important leads are. Unfortunately so many people ride without understanding how their horse moves that the simple secret of leads has become confusing to many riders. Once you figure out how the horse moves in the canter and how he gets on one "lead" or the other, the mystery of leads will clear up easily.

The canter is hard for some people to understand because it is difficult to see the horse's legs move at such a speed. Not only is the horse moving faster, but the horse's legs don't move in pairs, so there are four legs to watch instead of just two. If you learn how the legs move before you try to see them at work, it may help you to see the movements of the canter.

The canter is a three-beat gait which uses diagonal pairs of legs, two legs together and two separately. The first beat of the stride is one hind leg (first beat), then the opposite diagonal pair in unison (second beat), and finally the opposite foreleg (third beat). For instance: the right hind leg in support, then the left hind and right fore, then the left fore. This completes a cantering stride. The left fore, in this case, is the "leading" leg; the horse is on the "left lead." When a horse canters, he "leads" with one side or the other. The leading side quite clearly moves a little ahead of the other. This helps to balance the horse while he is turning. When traveling on a circle, the horse should lead with the inside leg: left lead when going to the left, etc. You can see a lead while watching a cantering horse by watching his forelegs. The leading side will advance ahead of the other side at each stride. If you're behind a cantering horse or where you can't see the front legs clearly, you can see the lead by determining which hind foot the horse pushes off with. You can see the lead while riding by watching the horse's shoulders: the leading shoulder advances further than the other. The horse also cants his body slightly when cantering so that the leading side is slightly turned toward the direction of the lead. However, the degree of cant should be kept to a minimum. Some horses canter almost sideways, making it easy to tell which lead they're on, but this should be discouraged.

It is important to remember that the cantering stride is begun with the hind legs, and that it is the hind leg, not the front, that determines which lead the horse takes. An experienced rider can feel the horse push off with the hind leg and can tell if the horse has taken the correct lead even before the horse has completed the first cantering stride. You can help the horse take the correct lead by making sure that he has his body in position to push off with the hind leg opposite the lead you want. This will be discussed more fully in the chapter on Problems Under Saddle.

The gallop, which is a full run, is a canter broken into four beats. The sequence of beats is the same except that the second beat is divided into two, with the hind foot striking the ground just before the fore foot. In both the canter and the gallop there is a period of suspension during the stride when the horse has all four feet off the ground. This occurs between the last beat of one stride and the first beat of another. This is the instant when a change of lead can occur without breaking stride.

Somewhere in this book you are undoubtedly expecting me to tell you never to lose your temper with your horse. I feel that this is not only unrealistic, it probably isn't even possible. There are times when you do lose control and get just plain mad at your horse. Think back to the last time this happened and try to remember what your horse did. If getting mad made the problem you were having worse, then your horse is not the type that can take an explosion of temper from you. In this case, you should probably try to control yourself. However, if getting mad improved the situation and made your horse respond to you, this should tell you something. While it doesn't mean that you should get mad all of the time, it may mean that you normally aren't firm enough with your horse and that he thinks he can get away with things. If you become more forceful with your signals normally, you may not have to get mad anymore!

If you take the time and have the patience to pay attention to your horse, you will find that riding becomes much easier and much more challenging. Learning how the horse moves, how to sit properly, give signals definitely and with the correct timing, and keeping the horse from developing undesirable habits, can turn your time on horseback into rewarding, enjoyable time. Your horse will become a much more pleasant animal to be around. Your horse is your friend, and he can be a loyal and charming companion indeed.

CHAPTER **2**

Preparing to Ride

Before you go for a ride, there are certain things you should do to get your horse ready. You should brush his back, around his girth area, his head, and his legs below the knees and hocks. This keeps dirt and balls of hair or burrs from rubbing the horse where the tack lies. Brushing the legs keeps thorns or stickers from scratching his legs and keeps caked mud and manure from making sore spots where his fetlock joints bend.

After you have groomed the horse at least this much, check his mouth and chin for sores that you may have missed the last time you rode. Check his back for cuts, lumps, or sores (in the winter when the coat is long, feel through it in case there is a cut or bruise you can't see). Also check for lameness by leading your horse around at a walk and trot a few times.

The final preparation you should make is to clean his feet out. This may seem a minor thing, since he often knocks the dirt out when you start riding anyway, but it can prevent a stone bruise if there are rocks or pebbles imbedded in the dirt in his feet.

Now you are ready to "tack up." It's generally easier to saddle the horse first while he's tied or standing with the lead line dangling (if he's been taught to "ground tie"). Have your tack out and ready before you bring the horse out so you don't have to leave him tied. Shake the pad or blanket out before you use it and check for burrs, twigs, or other things that might irritate the horse's back. Lay the blanket or pad on the horse's back far enough forward so the front of it is about halfway up his neck. If it's a blanket that is folded, place the folded edge to the front. Slide the blanket back until it is in the place where the saddle will

Placing the pad is very important when saddling, as a crooked or wrinkled pad may cause saddle sores. Place the pad forward of where it should lie and then slide it back so the hair on the back lies flat.

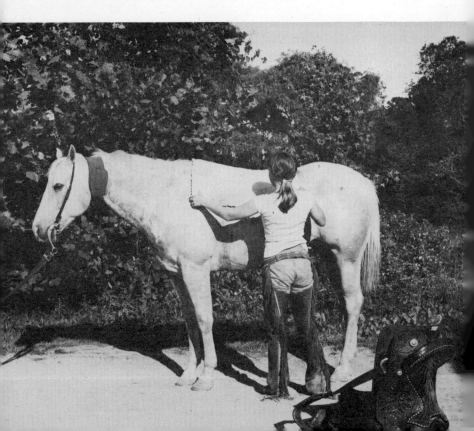

Check to see if the pad is centered on the back before you put the saddle on.

go. If it is fly season you may have to hold the pad in place while you put the saddle on as the horse will be shaking his skin to knock the flies off.

Before you pick up the saddle make sure the stirrups and girth are out of the way. If it is an English saddle, run the stirrups up on the leathers. With a Western saddle, hook the right stirrup over the saddle horn or lay it across the seat. Lay the cinch (girth) over the saddle as well.

Pick the saddle up with your left hand under the pommel (front) and the right hand under the cantle (back). Lift the saddle and either set it on the horse's back or slide it up and onto his back, depending on how tall the horse

Try to put the saddle on gently. This may not be easy with a heavy Western saddle, but your horse will stand much more reliably for saddling if he doesn't get slapped on the back with thirty pounds of leather every day. If the horse won't stand for saddling, doing it in the stall for a while may help.

is. Don't drop the saddle onto his back or throw it onto him. He won't stand still for very many saddlings if you treat him like that.

Once the saddle is on, shift it around a little to settle it in the hollow just behind the horse's withers, but don't pull it and the blanket forward or you will rub the hair on his back the wrong way, causing sores.

Instead of pushing the stirrups and girth off the saddle and letting them swing down, walk around the horse and

After you have placed the saddle, loosen the pad over the withers slightly so it doesn't pinch the horse. You can do this by lifting the front of the saddle with one hand and pulling the pad up with the other. Remember to smooth the hair under the pad with your hand before girthing up. The pad should be loosened over the withers on an English saddle, too.

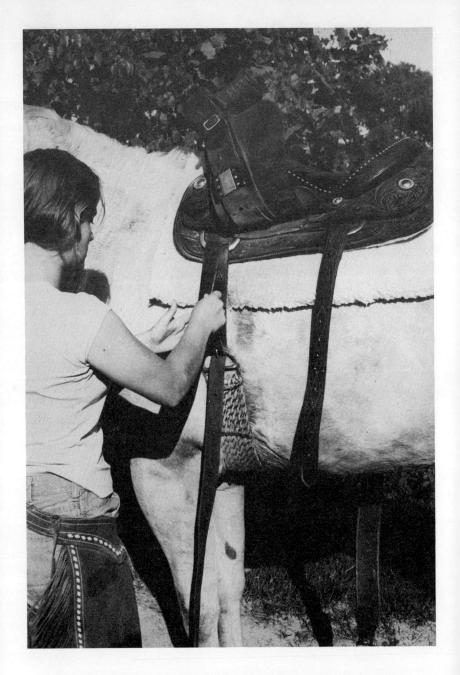

The girth on an English saddle is buckled in place, and on some Western saddles you can buckle the girth (or cinch) strap, as shown.

On most Western saddles, however, you must tie the cinch strap. To do this, thread the strap through the cinch ring and then through the ''dee'' ring on the saddle.

Cross the strap over and bring it back through the ring and down through the loop, like you were tying a necktie.

To tighten the cinch, pull up from the cinch ring and tighten the knot. It is easier to tie the knot when the cinch is fairly loose and then tighten it, than it is to tie it after you have tightened the cinch. Always check the tightness of the cinch or girth before you mount, as it may have loosened considerably as the horse relaxes.

On Western saddles with flank (rear) cinches, the flank cinch should be fastened only tight enough to keep from sliding around. A tight flank cinch may cause a horse to buck. Riders should bear in mind that a flank cinch serves no purpose other than in roping, when it holds the back of the sadddle down when the horse is holding the calf. Otherwise, it can be dispensed with.

This horse is standing patiently while the rider throws nearly 50 lbs. of saddle, stirrups and cinches flying, on him. Would your horse stand for this?

pull them down slowly. Straighten the girth carefully before you go back to tighten it. Fasten it so it is barely snug, then go back and check both sides to make sure it isn't twisted. When you have checked it, tighten it a little more. If you have a double-rigged Western saddle (with two cinches) you can now fasten the rear (flank) cinch. Adjust it so it just touches the horse's belly and is tight enough so he can't get a foot in it but is not too snug. A tight flank cinch may make a horse buck.

Now you are ready to bridle the horse. Many horses become almost impossible to bridle because their riders have been putting the bridle on incorrectly, and the horse learns to avoid being bridled by raising his head. Bridling correctly is easy once the technique is learned, and the right way to bridle is virtually foolproof, even on an uncooperative horse.

First sort out the bridle so that the reins aren't over the bit and the curb chain is either unhooked or held out of the way. You can loop the reins over the horse's neck to keep him from stepping on them, or lay them over your shoulder, whichever is easier for you.

Unhook the halter, take it off the horse's nose, and hook it again so it is hanging around the horse's neck. This will keep him from walking off. Take the crownpiece (top) of the bridle in your right hand and lay the bit (with the curb strap or chain out of the way) across the palm of your left hand. Stand on the left side of the horse's head, but not in front of him. Slowly bring the bridle up so your right hand is at the horse's forehead. Keep your left hand, holding the bit, under the horse's chin where he can't see it. If the horse moves his head, follow his movements without pulling on him until he stops. Wait until he is holding his head still before you do anything else.

When he has stopped arguing, gently bring the bit up to his lips. Slide your left thumb into the corner of his mouth and, as he opens his mouth in protest, slip the bit into his mouth. With practice this motion will become smooth and quick. Be careful not to bang the horse in the teeth with the bit. If the horse tosses his head, be patient and wait until he brings it back down before proceeding.

As the bit slides into the horse's mouth, use your right hand to pull the crownpiece up so you can let go of the bit and use both hands to sort out the ears, mane, and bridle at the horse's poll. Pull the headstall over the horse's ears carefully too; some horses are very sensitive about their ears.

Preparing to bridle, the rider holds the horse by the reins around the neck.

The horse resists as the bridle is brought up to his head, but if the rider waits, he will lower it and accept the bit. Don't try to bridle the horse in a hurry.

With the left hand holding the headstall over the forehead, bring the bit up below the horse's chin to the mouth. Most horses will open the mouth when the bit touches their teeth, but you may need to slip your thumb in the corner of the mouth to make your horse open up. Don't bang the bit against the horse's teeth to make him take the bit, or he will surely raise his head.

When the bit slides into the horse's mouth, pull the headstall over the horse's ear on the side closest to you, taking care not to let the bit fall out of his mouth.

Then slip the headstall over the horse's other ear and straighten the mane under the bridle. If the horse is very fussy about his ears, you may need to unbuckle the headstall and put it on without slipping it back over the ears. If the horse is hard to bridle, bridling in the stall is recommended.

If the bridle has a noseband, you may want to unbuckle it while you put the bridle on, at least until you get the hang of it. When the bridle is on, straighten the browband and noseband, if it has them, and fasten the throatlatch. Adjust it so that it is loose enough to get your hand through. This will keep it from cutting into the horse's neck when he flexes his head at the poll. After you have fastened the throatlatch, check the curb chain or strap and fasten if necessary. The curb strap or chain should lie in the hollow of the horse's chin and should be loose enough to slip two fingers through. It should not be so tight that it acts on the horse when the reins are slack, since this may teach the horse to ignore its action, as he will get no reward for responding to a pull on the mouth.

If you bridle correctly, and do it gently, your horse should never be hard to bridle. Always try to take your time when bridling, since it is easy to get rough without realizing it when you're in a hurry.

Once the bridle is on, put the reins over the horse's head. Before you untie him, however, check your girth again, as it will probably be a little looser than before.

Now you can untie the horse and lead him around for a few steps to let everything settle and to let the girth loosen up a little more if the horse relaxes again. When you are ready to get on, pull the stirrups down and check your girth one more time. Have a good ride!

CHAPTER 3

Where to Ride

Before you actually mount and begin to ride, it would be wise to consider where to go. If you have a small piece of property with barely enough room for a stable and paddock, as many horse owners do, you may have a problem. Or you may have a stable and a pasture which takes up the rest of your land, except the lawn. This leaves you with just a small pen or your pasture to ride in.

Two things should be remembered when considering where to ride. It is asking for trouble to ride in the horse's pasture, and it is not a good idea to ride in the same place every time you ride. A horse considers his pasture his own domain. He tends to take liberties there that he would not outside, and since he is usually close to the barn or at least within sight of it he will have a tendency to want to head for the stable all of the time. Also, he may have favorite spots in the pasture that he might want to go to. Therefore it is better if you can arrange to have somewhere else to ride, and use the pasture only occasionally. You may be able to find a neighbor who has a field you could use, or a patch of woods you could make trails in (sometimes the trails are already there in the form of old roads). A nearby park or state forest should come in handy, provided that you check with the ranger for permission. He can tell you which trails you can use and which are out of bounds. He can also tell you how to tell the boundaries of the park or forest so you don't wander out, and can even give you a map of the trails and roads so you don't get lost.

As for riding along the highway, I would not advise riding along it except for short distances, unless it has wide, grassy shoulders and plenty of places to get off the road far enough to let motorcycles or other spooky vehicles by. When I was a child we rode along the highway most of the time, but traffic is heavier now and there is too much trash along the shoulder.

If no one around you is cooperative about letting you use their land for riding, and there are no places other than your own small pasture to ride, you may be wise to find a place to board your horse that has riding areas. If you have a trailer, you may be able to get a stable to allow you to use their riding facilities, for cleaning stalls or other compensation, if necessary.

If your space at home is very limited, you should definitely make an effort to find somewhere else besides your own yard or paddock to ride at least part of the time, as your horse will become bored and sulky from being ridden in the same place all of the time.

CHAPTER 4

Basic Horsemanship

Learning to ride really well takes years of experience, and it is important to have an instructor to help you start riding correctly. However, even without someone to watch you ride and guide you, you can learn to ride safely and well. Riding correctly involves learning to sit right, developing a sense of balance and rhythm with the horse, and giving signals correctly and with the right timing. From there on, it is a matter of enforcing commands firmly but not roughly and learning to cope with problems and disobedience as they arise.

This chapter will try to give you a basis with which to begin learning to ride safely, without going into too much detail on form. Many people ride quite well without being what you would call "show riders"; that is, they don't have the polish and professional look of a show rider, yet they handle their horses well and enjoy riding. Anyone, no matter how unathletic or overweight, can learn to ride well enough to enjoy it and to be a safe rider, provided that they have a suitable horse.

Mounting is one of those things that is difficult for the short person or someone who is overweight, and it is also a problem for a small child with a full-sized horse. One solution to the problem is to use a mounting block, but it is a good idea to learn to mount from the ground as well, since there are times when there is no block or even a fallen tree to use. Also, not all horses will stand still next to a block while you clamber aboard.

When you are ready to get on, check your girth. Always do this before you mount, no matter who put the saddle on or how many times you have already checked it. Simply put two fingers under the front edge and pull. Tighten it until it is just snug enough to keep the saddle from slipping when you mount, but not so tight that it feels like a girdle to the horse. A horse with a very round back and low, flat withers usually needs the girth a little tighter than one with high withers and a narrow back. You should not depend on the girth to keep the saddle from slipping no matter what; your own balance is the most important factor in keeping it from turning under the horse's belly.

It is also a good idea to check the stirrups to make sure that they are the same length. To do this, stand in front of the horse and see if they are hanging evenly. Make sure the horse is standing straight since it will make the stirrups appear uneven if he is resting one hind foot. You can check the stirrups for length before you get on by putting your fingertips at the top of the stirrup leather and pulling the stirrup up to your armpit with the other hand. If the stirrup is just as long as your arm, it is at least close to the correct length for you.

You should check the bridle and curb strap before mounting, and check the horse's feet. Clean them out if necessary, and check for loose shoes, protruding horseshoe nails, and cracks in the hooves. If he has any of these problems, don't ride the horse until you get the blacksmith to correct them.

If you have been having trouble getting your horse to move away from the barn after you get on, lead him away from the stable before you mount. Make a habit of varying the place of mounting from day to day so he doesn't get used to having one spot to stop and stand. It is a good idea to mount next to a fence if you have trouble getting on, so you can face the fence to cut down on the risk of the

If your horse has not been ridden lately, or has been kept in the stall or is otherwise extra energetic, longeing him a little before riding may be wise. This will enable him to work off any bucks and foolishness before you get on. This is especially useful with young horses which are prone to shenanigans anyway. If your horse will not work in a circle around you on a line, turning him loose in a small paddock for half an hour or so before riding may serve the same purpose.

horse walking off while you are halfway on. Or you can ask someone to hold the horse while you mount until you have mastered the technique.

Before you start to mount, put the reins over the horse's head and gather them up enough so you could pull him up if he tried to move ahead, but not so tight that he wants to back up. If he has a habit of turning his head and trying to nip, shorten the rein on the other side.

One of the recommended ways of mounting is to stand so you are facing the horse's hindquarters, so you are thrown into the saddle if the horse moves forward while you get on. However, this may be impossible for you to

Before mounting, gather your reins so they are short enough that you can pull the horse up should he try to move. Make sure the horse is settled and standing quietly before you try to get on.

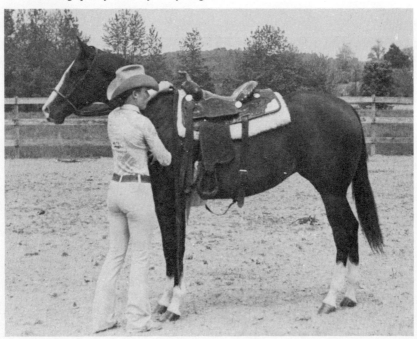

The most widely accepted stance for mounting, especially in English riding, is to stand at the horse's shoulder facing his hindquarters.

accomplish if the horse is very tall, or if you are very short-legged, or otherwise unable to get on easily. Also, this stance prevents you from watching the horse's head while you mount, which keeps you from being able to tell by his ears and general expression if he is about to kick, bite, or move away. Therefore, I recommend that you stand next to the stirrup facing the side of the horse. Another alternative is to stand behind the stirrup facing the horse's head. This is the least safe way to mount, as you would be left hopping along on one foot if the horse stepped forward, but it may be the only way some people can mount at all.

If you have trouble reaching the stirrup, you may want to let it down a few notches for mounting, and learn to

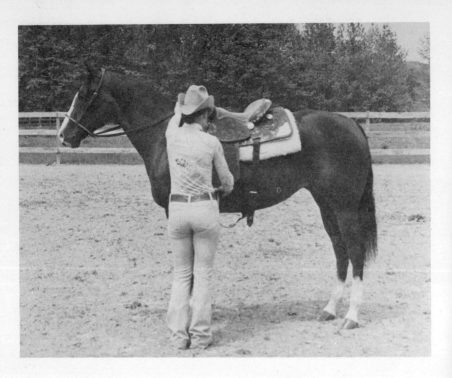

Another method, which enables you to watch the horse's head and gauge his reactions to what is going on, is to stand next to the saddle.

adjust after you have gotten on. There is also an exercise that helps stretch your leg muscles so that you can develop more reach for the stirrup. This exercise can be done in the house or next to a fence. Stand next to a low table or the fence and put one foot on it not too high off the ground (about two feet). Walk your other foot backwards as far as you can so you are stretching the muscles in the backs of your legs. Then lean down over your knee as far as you can, until it hurts. Do this for several days using a low table or board in the fence, then gradually increase the height of the raised foot until it is waist height or above. You will be amazed at how much farther you can reach,

The third way, which is more awkward but the only way some people can manage to get on at all, is to face the horse's head. The disadvantage to this is that the rider would be left hopping along if the horse moved forward, and it is harder to control the horse from this angle.

and at the overall improvement in the strength of your legs. The effects of this exercise last practically forever.

Now, back to the horse, which we left standing somewhere! Standing on the left side of the horse, gather the reins and grab a handful of mane with your left hand (reins in this hand, too). Do not hold the pommel or saddle horn, as you are likely to pull the saddle over if you do. Put your foot in the stirrup, using your right hand to guide it. Then move your right hand to the pommel or horn if you can reach it, or to the cantle if you can't. The trick to mounting with ease, or at least without a ridiculous

As the rider begins to mount, the horse wants to move. The left hand on the reins prevents the horse from moving off.

amount of effort and pulling the horse over at the same time, is to push yourself up with your right leg, instead of pulling yourself up with your hands. Count to three and give a tremendous push with your foot, while pulling with your hands at the same time. This should be a much easier way to mount, since your legs are stronger than your arms.

If your horse starts to move off while you are halfway on, you should get off and start again, rather than just hopping on fast and then stopping him. He should be taught to stand until you are completely mounted and settled.

The horse that backs away from the rider can be backed into a corner of the fence until he learns to stand. If worse

This young horse shows her resistance to being mounted by leaning back slightly. The rider mounts slowly, keeping the reins short but not tight. Too tight a rein would make the horse back up. When you mount, always land gently.

comes to worst, you can try mounting in the stall for a while. Some ex-racehorses find the confines of their stalls soothing and will stand better inside.

Problems with the horse moving around while being mounted are usually caused by the rider in the first place. If you are poking the horse in the side with your foot as you get on, you may have to change your stance so your foot is turned sideways and doesn't poke him. If you are pulling the saddle over so hard that it hurts the horse's back, try using the mane instead of the saddle horn or pommel. If you are very heavy, you might have to use a

Once mounted, make the horse stand still while you sort out your reins, find the stirrups, and generally get settled. If the horse won't stand still for mounting, mounting next to the fence or in the stall will help teach him to be still.

mounting block or get a stronger horse. Some horses become restless when mounted because the rider comes down with a thump when he gets on. Practice easing down into the saddle more gently. Also make sure that you sit still for a minute or two before you ask the horse to move off so that he doesn't anticipate this and try to move too soon.

You may find that your horse doesn't stand well no matter where you try to get on. In this case you may have to get someone to hold him for you until he gets better about this. Have the person stand on his right side to keep him from moving forward or swinging his hindquarters away from you. Have them hold the reins behind the bit, rather than the headstall of the bridle. Practicing the "Whoa" command to give the horse extra practice at responding to it will help, too.

Once you are mounted, learn to find your right stirrup without having to bend down for it. When you are on and have both stirrups, lean over in your right stirrup for a moment to straighten the saddle on the horse's back. Otherwise you may ride the whole time sitting lopsided on him, which can give him a sore back, and will also interfere with both his balance and yours.

Now that you are on, how do you sit? Your ideal in riding is to interfere as little as possible with the horse's natural movements, while still getting him to do as you wish. Generally the best seat to use to achieve this is to sit naturally, upright, and in the middle of the saddle. Your legs should hang fairly straight, with some angle at the hips and knees. Your feet should be more or less directly under your hips. This way you can use your lower leg to give signals to the horse without having to move it backwards very far, if at all, and your thigh is in contact with the saddle for grip when needed. Your arms should hang naturally to the elbows and then follow a more or less straight line from the elbow through your hands to the bit. This is true for both English and Western riding. In this book I will discuss the two almost as if they were one. I will not go into the different kinds of seat in English riding (forward seat, hunt seat, saddle, etc.), but will discuss a general seat that can be applied to all types of riding. Those who wish to show should study the various seats used in their classes and should probably employ a riding instructor to polish their form, as it is very difficult to achieve "show polish" without help.

Your posture on the horse is very important. This rider is sitting erect, with hands and legs in good position. This is good form for both English and Western riding.

Your posture on your horse is very important. It should generally be upright, although you should lean slightly forward as your horse's speed increases.

As you ride you give signals to your horse to communicate your wishes to him. These are called *aids*. One aid is your voice, which you can use at any time to give specific commands, or to soothe or quiet an uneasy horse. Voice commands intended to encourage the horse to speed up should be given with a rising inflection in a firm, although not necessarily loud, voice. Words to calm or slow down should be given in a soothing, quiet tone. A voice command should always be reinforced by a physical aid if the horse

Slouching in the saddle with legs too far forward not only looks bad, but puts you off balance and out of touch with your horse. The rider's weight is too far back, and her legs are so far forward she can't give proper leg signals. This type of seat also encourages the hands to come up too high.

does not respond to it. The horse then learns to respond to the voice in order to avoid the physical contact.

Another aid is the rider's hands. Because your hands pull the bit against the sensitive bars of the horse's mouth, you can inflict great pain with them. Therefore, you should always use as gentle a pressure as you can get the horse to respond to, and should never yank the horse's mouth roughly.

The hands give turning, slowing, and stopping signals. They are also used to give checking signals, to warn the

Form at the trot (or jog, shown here) remains basically the same. At an English trot, which is faster, the rider could lean slightly forward. The rider's hands in this picture are a little too high.

Form at the canter (lope). Nothing changes drastically, but the body is inclined forward somewhat. This does not mean that the rider should lean over the horse's neck, but should lean *slightly* forward. As the horse naturally raises his head at the lope, the rider's hands can also rise, but only slightly.

horse of impending actions, and to get the horse's attention. The art of reining is complicated and a rider never stops learning how to improve his communication through the bit. The guidelines given here are general ones, and the rider is encouraged to develop his own "language" of the bit with his horse. You should keep in mind, however, that the pressure you exert should be as light as possible, and that you must always reward obedience by the horse with a release of pressure, even if it is only for a stride or two.

For most pleasure riding, riding on a slightly slack rein most of the time is probably best. As you become more experienced and get into more complicated maneuvers such as Western reining patterns or elementary dressage, you can begin to ride "on contact," where you have a constant feel of the horse's mouth.

The general "rule" for turning calls for the English rider to use one hand on each rein, pulling on the right rein for a right turn, etc. The Western rider is expected to use one hand, pulling his hand to the left and laying the right rein against the neck for a left turn (neck-reining). However,

When the rider gives the horse a stopping signal, the hands should be pulled back toward the hips, not up. Pulling up causes the horse to raise his head.

Turning signals are given in two ways. Direct reining, used in English riding, can also be used in Western riding. In fact, most riders should probably forget all about "neckreining" and ride with two hands, as it is usually less confusing to the horse. In this picture a young horse is being taught to turn properly by the use of a low, wide hand in direct reining. The horse is taught to follow his nose, which keeps him in balance and enables him to turn more quickly and more gracefully.

the average horse responds best to either a combination of the two types of reining, or to the English direct reining. Except for riding in shows, where one hand is required, there is no reason why a Western rider can't ride with both hands, and vice-versa. A rider should be prepared to use two hands if necessary to get the horse to respond, and you will soon learn which kind or kinds of reining give you the best control.

If you ride with one hand, it doesn't matter which hand you use. I suspect that most riders use the left hand since they already have the reins in this hand when they mount. Working cowboys use their left hand to rein so they can handle the rope with their right hand. The best place to put your free hand is probably on your leg just above the knee. It is out of the way there but still in a place where you can "grab leather" if necessary, or put two hands on the reins quickly. You can also rest your free hand against your stomach just above the belt, if it is comfortable. Avoid waving it around as you ride, since this will interfere with your balance and may distract your horse. You can hold the ends of the reins in your free hand, keeping them against your leg to keep them from slapping against the horse's shoulder.

Your hands should be in front of you when you ride, not wandering out to the side. They should stay relatively close to the front of the saddle, moving somewhat forward when the speed of the horse increases and you lean forward. Some people claim that carrying the hands too high (above the horn in a Western saddle) encourages the horse to raise his head, but unless the reins are kept too tight, this isn't necessarily true. A low pull on the reins (with the hands below the hips) tends to make the horse pull against the bit by poking his nose out, which is undesirable. However, a backwards and upwards pull causes the horse to want to

Neckreining, the old Western favorite, is fine when done correctly, and when the horse knows how to neckrein, but improper neckreining pulls the horse's head the wrong way for the turn and makes the horse fight the bit.

Proper hand position is nearly touching the horse's neck in front of the saddle. When the horse's speed increases, and when jumping, stopping, or turning is about to be done, the hands should move forward beside the neck and the reins shortened so the hands do not come back to the rider's lap when he uses them.

tuck his chin, if the pull is timed properly. Of course, steady pulling for no reason, or too rough a pull, will pull the horse's head out of position or cause him to resist anyway, no matter which direction the pull comes from or where the rider's hands are.

The rider's hands should not rise much above the belt line, however, as an excessively high pull may pull the horse's nose up. A rider with a very high-headed horse may find that it helps to lower his hands, especially if the horse

Hands too high draw the horse's head out of position. If the hands start out too high, pulling the reins only makes them go higher, which results in a high-headed horse.

tends to overflex (tucks his chin too much). Usually, however, the solution to the high-headed horse is to use less pressure on the mouth.

When you pull the rein for a turn, bring your arm straight back to keep from pulling the horse's head too far to the side. The exception to this rule is when the horse resists a turn, when you may have to pull your hand out to the side and "strong arm" him around.

Many of your signals are given with your legs: turning signals, signals to increase speed or change gait, and even signals to slow down. The principle of leg aids is that the horse tends to move away from pressure on his side. Thus when the horse is moving and you squeeze with your leg, he tends to move forward away from the leg.

While most riders use both legs together to give signals to speed up, you may find your horse responds better to one leg at a time. Many horses are trained to respond to both legs together for a walk and trot, and one leg for a canter. Generally the rider uses the leg away from the direction of the turn to give a turning signal, although some horses respond better to the inside leg. Some experimenting with your horse should enable you to decide which signals to use for him. If he doesn't seem to understand any leg signals, you may need to teach him leg aids. This can be done by teaching the turn on the forehand, which is explained later.

While a rider can tell the horse many things with his legs, his body (seat) can speak even more clearly. The seat is the strongest aid the rider has, although many people are unaware that they even have this aid. The seat has the most effect on the horse because he can feel every shift of your weight clearly. A very small rider on a large horse is at a great disadvantage then, because the horse is not influenced by the weight of the rider. This explains why

The rider's legs, in addition to giving signals for more speed, also should be used for turning. The rider here is using her outside leg to turn the horse away from her leg. Some horses respond better to the inside leg behind the girth, to move the hindquarters around. Use of the legs in turning helps keep the horse light on the forehand by encouraging him to use his hindquarters.

a horse will take a child back to the barn every time, yet behaves perfectly well for an adult rider. The horse just doesn't get all the signals from the child, no matter how well he or she rides.

You can use your seat as a signal in many ways, and every other signal you give should be accompanied by a body signal ("body English"). The rider should "push" the horse forward with his seat when he wishes to increase his speed, lean slightly into the turns, and shift his weight back slightly to slow down. The seat should become passive (non-influencing) when the horse is moving at the desired pace.

The rider's seat is a very important aid. The driving seat is used here for getting the horse into a lope. Compare with the next picture.

The rider, once the horse is in a lope, relaxes the back and assumes a passive seat. Note the more relaxed attitude of rider as compared with the last picture.

All of your signals should be timed to help each other out, rather than confusing the horse by cross-signaling. Care should be taken so that the rider does not give a squeeze with the legs for speed and then pull on the mouth to slow down at the same time. This kind of treatment produces a horse that carries his nose in the air, tends to rear or balk, and is generally nervous and unhappy. This is one of the most common faults in the beginning rider who has no supervision.

Once you are mounted and settled in the saddle, check to make sure that your stirrups are the right length. If your legs seem to have too much bend at the knees (knees are too high) or seem cramped, the stirrups are too short; if you have to reach for them or can't get your heels down, they are too long. A good length for most people is just at the bottom of your foot when your legs are hanging relaxed.

When you ride, try to stay relaxed enough so that your hips rock back and forth with the motion of the horse. You can emphasize this rocking to encourage the horse to move faster (driving seat), and set your back against the motion when you want to slow down (bracing back). If you ride so stiffly that you never move your back with the horse's motion, he will learn to ignore your seat and back aids completely, as he gets no reward (relaxing the back) when he goes well.

Sometimes horses respond to completely different signals than they are supposed to, but generally horses are trained to obey a fairly standard set of signals. What follows is the method of signals I have found to be effective on a majority of horses.

The rider starts the horse into a walk by giving a slight push forward with the seat and applying a light push or squeeze with one or both legs just behind the girth. (If your legs are in the right position this can be accomplished with little, if any, leg motion.) This signal can be accompanied by the voice command "Walk!" Before starting off the rider should make sure that his reins are short enough to make contact with the horse's mouth with a minimum of hand motion by the rider. He should "gather" the reins again before each increase in gait since the horse raises his head when he speeds up. If the reins are left too loose the rider cannot pull on the horse's mouth when he needs to without a lot of hauling up of excess rein. However, if he keeps the reins too tight, the horse may get so

Finding the correct rein length is somtimes hard to do, yet it is very important. Here the horse has freedom of head movement, yet the reins are short enough that the rider can use them without moving the hands very far.

he ignores the pressure, or he may become a nervous wreck, depending on how sensitive his mouth is. Some riders keep the reins tight all the time because they think the horse will surely run away if they loosen them. They usually find, however, that if they let the reins out just enough, the horse will begin to relax and slow down rather than try to take off. If the horse finds no relief of pressure on his mouth by slowing down, he may try to outrun the pain, not being able to reason out that the bit is inescapable. Many "runaways" are caused by the rider's using too much bit on a nervous horse and keeping a tight rein. Give your horse a chance to work on slightly loose reins, ride with a calm, relaxed attitude, and keep the work fairly slow to determine whether a tight rein is really necessary.

If your horse hangs his head down and feels like he would drop it completely if you didn't hold it up, let your reins loosen by moving your hands forward. Once your horse realizes you won't hold his head up for him he'll raise it to a normal level again.

When you ask your horse for a trot (or whatever gait he uses instead), remember that he will raise his head a little, so shorten your reins a few inches. This does not mean that you should tighten them, but rather move your hands forward up the reins so that you have the same degree of tightness but less rein between the horse's mouth and your hands. Keeping your reins too long may make it impossible for you to retain control should he do something unexpected (shy at something, for instance).

As you prepare to increase your speed, you will have to shift your weight forward slightly to match your horse's increase. He will momentarily shift his weight to his hindquarters to push off into the trot, then settle into a rhythmical gait. If you do not balance yourself properly, you will be "left behind" when he starts up. To ask for a trot, lean forward slightly and give a light squeeze with one or both legs (use the calf of your leg). Give a squeeze at first, and use more force if the horse does not respond. Avoid kicking the horse with your heels. This not only looks amateurish, but also throws you off balance. In the long run, it is not as effective as a well-timed squeeze anyway. Give leg signals with alternating leg movements, timed to the horse's strides. Remember to reward the horse for speeding up (even if it's only a little) by relaxing the signal for a stride or two. Eventually your horse will learn to respond to a light squeeze to avoid a stronger one.

If your horse seems to ignore leg signals, try using a crop or switch just behind your leg to reinforce them. Make sure you give the horse a chance to respond to the leg before using the crop, however, so he has a choice of which signal to obey. Otherwise he will never learn to obey the leg, and you will always have use the crop.

Don't surprise the horse by thumping on him suddenly and scaring him into a trot. This isn't fair to him and it will throw you off balance when he jumps forward. Warn him of the change in pace by gathering your reins and shifting your weight forward, then ease calmly into the trot. Use only as much force as is necessary. Of course, if your horse is very sluggish and unresponsive, you may have to resort to very strong signals.

When you give signals to speed up, always make sure you are not pulling on the horse's mouth at the same time. An advanced rider on an advanced horse may use the leg and hand signals at the same time, and you may read about this in other books. The beginning rider should never pull and kick at the same time. It takes years of training and experience before a horse and rider are ready for the delicate timing of signals that is involved with riding on contact and in collection. For the average inexperienced rider, pulling and kicking at the same time will produce a horse that either doesn't respond to any signals at all or over-responds to everything. It can lead to problems such as tossing the head, rearing, bolting, and balking.

If the horse starts off into too fast a trot, give him a few strides to settle down before you pull him back. Pulling him down as soon as he starts trotting may confuse him. Often a horse will start off too fast and then settle into a reasonable pace on his own. You may have given him too strong a signal and caused him to jump into too fast a gait.

At the trot, your hands should not go up and down with

your body as you post. Relax your arms and let your hands stay down near the horse's neck. Keep your reins fairly short, but not so tight that you pull the horse's head up and down as you post. At a walk and canter your hands can move back and forth with the nodding motion of the horse's head, but they should stay still at a trot.

Remember that you should be balanced over your feet so that if the horse disappeared from under you, you would land on your feet. This does not mean that you should stand in your stirrups, but that you should sit on the saddle with your feet under your hips. It takes some experimenting to learn how much pressure to put in your stirrups and how to sit to achieve this balance. Eventually you will learn to feel when you are off balance and you will automatically adjust yourself to keep it. In the beginning it is helpful to have someone to tell you when you look "behind" the horse, too far forward, or when your legs are swinging back and forth.

Whether you ride English or Western, it is handy to learn to post. Once you have learned to sit a slow trot comfortably and without losing your balance, it is time to learn this. For some people posting seems to come naturally and they may learn it accidentally while trying to learn to sit the trot. Others may have to make a conscious effort to find the posting rhythm. Whichever type of rider you are, you will find it helpful to relax and let the horse throw you into the rhythm. As the horse brings the diagonal pairs of legs forward, his back rises with first one pair and then the other. When you post, you rise and fall with one set of legs. This eliminates half of the bounces of the trot.

There are various ways to learn to post. One is to practice going up and down in your stirrups at a standstill, then at a walk, and finally at a trot, eventually synchronizing your movement with that of the horse. Another is to

Posting, on the right diagonal. The rider rises as the right diagonal pair of legs (right front and left rear) come forward.

Posting, right diagonal, sitting as the right front leg comes back.

trot the horse and try to relax as much as possible, concentrating on feeling the rhythm of the strides until you can rise and fall with them. Then you can tighten your knees and thighs a little until you can iron out the extra bumps and rise and fall smoothly. You should soon find this rhythm and in a few rides you will probably be posting all the time. Of course English riders post the trot most of the time, and Western riders traditionally sit the slow trot, or jog, but there is no reason why Western riders can't post the trot when pleasure riding. You will probably find it is much more comfortable to post, especially if your horse has a rough trot.

When you have learned to walk and trot comfortably and with good control, including turns, hills, and stops, you are probably ready to try cantering.

At first it may be easier for you to canter from a trot. This does not mean, however, that you should trot the horse as fast as he can go and then force him into a gallop. This is hard on him and it will be easier for you to do it at a slower speed.

If possible, do your first cantering in a ring, paddock, or other enclosure. This will help keep your horse at reasonable speed, and will discourage him from running away if you should lose your balance and drop the reins. This will depend on your skill and your confidence in your horse's manners.

Prepare to canter from a slow trot. Gather your reins so they are fairly short, with your hands forward nearly halfway up the horse's neck. Your horse will both raise his head and bob it up and down when he canters and while you want the reins short for control, you don't want to pull his mouth at every stride. You may want to catch a lock of mane with one hand so you won't pull the reins if you lose your balance at first.

When you get ready to take the canter from a trot, stop posting and shift your weight slightly forward. Lean forward from the waist slightly. When the horse takes a canter his front end will come up more than usual and he will move forward with a slight burst of speed, which will tend to leave you behind.

If you are in a ring try to time your canter depart as you come out the curve. Outside a ring time it at the start of a straight stretch with a clear way ahead. This will give him time to get into the canter before having to negotiate a turn.

You should decide which lead you will ask the horse to take before you begin to canter. This is true even if you don't show your horse, because you don't want him to take the same lead all the time. If you allow him to take the same lead every time you canter, he will become one-sided, and you will have difficulty getting him to turn to the other direction.

If you are in the ring you want the horse to take the lead toward the inside of the circle. Give the cantering signal with the leg away from the lead you want; that is, the right leg for a left lead, etc. Try to give the signal when the horse is aligned properly, when he is traveling in a straight line (his body is straight following his head) or when his hindquarters are slightly more toward the center of the circle or toward the lead you want. This position helps him push off with the opposite hind leg, which is correct. One way to align the horse properly is to give a light pull on the outside rein while pushing his hindquarters over a little with your outside leg. Don't pull his head very far to the side, however, as this will pull him off balance. Don't lean over the horse's shoulder when you start into a canter to check the lead, as some riders do. This not only looks bad, but it also forces the horse's weight forward

Pushing the horse into a lope (canter) on the left lead. The horse pushes off with the right hind leg. Note the driving seat of the rider, and how her hands have come forward to give the horse more rein.

onto his forehand and makes it difficult for him to take the canter smoothly and quickly.

When you are ready to take the canter depart, stop posting, lean forward slightly, and give the horse a strong leg signal behind the girth on the opposite side from the lead you want. At the *same* time, give a definite pushing aid with your back and seat and make sure your hands move forward with the horse's head motion as he takes the canter. If your leg and body signals are timed correctly, the horse should go right into a canter. If they are not, he might simply trot faster. It will take some practice to

The horse steps into the second phase of the cantering stride, where the right front and left hind legs support. The horse's head is still high, and the rider keeps her hands forward.

get the canter depart on command if they are correct. If your horse won't take a canter at all, or only after a lot of fast, jouncy trotting strides, try to find someone who is an experienced rider to try it for you. If he can get the horse to canter, have him help you learn to make your signals more definite. The use of a crop along with your leg signal may also help.

If your horse is the quick, excitable type you may want to use less leg pressure and depend more on "body English." You can also use a voice command with the physical aids, or instead of them.

If your horse is reluctant to canter, make sure that you are not holding him too tightly. He will be afraid to move into a faster gait if he thinks you are going to yank him in the mouth, and you can hardly blame him. Loosen the reins by moving your hands forward when you give the cantering signals. Too tight a rein and indefinite or poorly timed signals are usually the causes of a poor canter depart. Once the horse takes a canter from a trot and you have learned to sit the canter comfortably, you can begin to take the canter from a walk, if you wish.

As the horse passes through the diagonal phase of the canter his weight moves forward to his forehand and his head comes down. The slack is being taken out of the reins as the left front (leading) leg meets the ground.

The third phase of the canter, leading leg in support. The horse's head has come down and is just coming back up as the body swings through the phase of support by the leading leg.

Now that you have learned some things about how to get your horse going, there are some techniques for slowing down and stopping that you should know. It seems to be much more difficult for the horse to understand stopping signals, even though he really does want to stop. I suspect that many of the problems that riders have with stopping arise from not giving the horse enough time to stop properly, and from lack of training of both the horse and the rider. It is quite possible to get quick, flashy stops from a horse, even from fast gaits, but this type of work takes years of training and experience to achieve. The average rider should probably forget about sliding stops and concentrate on getting his horse to stop calmly and in a relaxed manner when he is told to do so.

There are two keys to stopping: one is training, the other is balance. The basis of training to stop the horse is the word "Whoa" (pronounced "ho"). This voice command should be instilled in the horse from the day you buy him. It should be used in hand and under saddle, and you should start teaching it to the horse from the ground on the lead rope. If the horse really knows what "Whoa" means, you

The next phase of the canter is that of suspension. All four feet off the ground, the horse passes from one stride to the next. This is the instant when a flying change of leads can occur. In this picture the horse has just put the outside hind leg down to begin the next stride.

have a good start at getting him to stop on command when ridden.

In order to stop well under saddle, the horse must be able to balance himself. It is difficult for him to stop if the rider is leaning forward over his neck, and it confuses him to be asked to stop when the rider's seat is still driving him ahead. The rider should therefore practice using his seat while riding to drive the horse ahead when desired, and to stop and brace against the horse's movements when a stop is wanted.

When a horse is traveling at any gait faster than a walk, he has to bring his hindquarters farther up under him in order to come to a stop. If the rider doesn't give the horse enough warning before he gives a stopping signal, the horse will have to take several more strides to gather himself before he can stop.

There are several ways to get a horse to set himself up for a stop. One is the "driving the horse up to the bit" method that is discussed in most horse books. This is the method used to get a well-trained horse working on the bit (on contact) to give a smooth, quick stop, but it is usually beyond the ability of the average pleasure rider. The other method that gets good results with an average horse used to working on fairly loose reins is one which can be mastered easily, and is less apt to confuse the horse. Several strides before you want to stop, check the horse slightly with a short pull on the reins. This gives a warning that you are going to stop. Count to three after the check, then give the voice command "Whoa" and brace your back against the horse's forward motion at the same time. This will give you a feeling of sitting down and back on the saddle while pushing on the stirrups with your feet. If you also freeze your hand(s), this should bring enough pressure on the bit to get the message across without pulling too hard. This method must be taught to the horse

Setting up for a stop from a lope (canter). If the signal is properly timed, and the horse is responsive enough, a complete stop can be achieved from a canter with no trotting strides. In this picture the horse is in the proper position to stop correctly, with the hind legs well under the body.

If the rider were to give the horse a signal to stop at this moment, he would have to either break the cantering stride to arrange his feet properly to stop, or complete the cantering stride before he could stop.

gradually, starting at a walk and progressing to faster gaits as each speed is mastered. Its success depends largely on the timing of your signals and how well the horse responds to the voice command. Over a period of time the horse should learn to respond quickly to this, if you are consistent with your signals.

If you have difficulty getting your horse to understand these signals, or if he just doesn't seem to be able to stop within a dozen or so strides of your commands, using a visual aid may help. This means riding the horse up to something large and solid like the fence or barn until he realizes that he will have to stop, and then signaling for it. This may help get the idea across and teach him to gather himself as well. The only disadvantage to this is that it may encourage him to turn sideways as he stops, which is undesirable. If he tries to turn, use your legs and reins to keep him straight, and don't pressure him as much. He will stop straight if he is given enough time to set himself up properly.

If the horse throws his head up on the stops, you are using too much rein pressure. Also, make sure you release the pressure on his mouth as soon as he begins to stop in order to reward him.

If the horse is asked to stop too abruptly for his ability, or if too harsh a signal is used, he may throw his head up like this. Working gradually up to stops from a lope is advised, starting with walking and jogging.

When the horse has stopped, reward him by standing still for at least a few moments, and by a pat and a nice word. The use of rewards in riding is infinitely more important than punishments, if you wish to have a pleasant, cooperative horse.

Once you have mastered the basics of riding, or at least are progressing without exciting your horse or making him throw his head around, you will find that most of these things will become second nature to you and that you won't have to think about them anymore. Don't worry if changing your riding style makes your legs sore at first. Once you have trained the proper muscles they will no longer bother you and you will be more comfortable in the long run. When you are riding in balance and with the proper amount of control, you will be surprised at how easy it becomes.

Remember, if riding is work and worry, you are doing something wrong! When things go smoothly and both you and the horse are happy and comfortable, you are doing well, even if you don't look stylish. Cooperation and friendship between horse and rider are more important than looking "just so" and having to fight the horse to get him to perform as sometimes is the case.

CHAPTER 5

Trail Riding

If you are lucky enough to have plenty of woods around your home, or even a State Forest, you may spend most or all of your time on horseback in trail riding. One of the first things to remember is not to overtax either your horse or yourself. If you only ride once or twice a week, don't expect your horse to be able to go out for the whole day at a fast pace. On a long ride, keep the pace to a walk most of the time. You can usually tell how much to work the horse without overtiring him by how tired you are getting. When you get tired and sore, you can assume the horse is too, and it is time to quit. By the same token, if you are sore the next day, so is the horse, so don't expect him to go out and win ribbons in a show, or to go on another long ride.

Short rides can be taken at a faster pace, although you should avoid riding an unconditioned horse at a trot or canter for long periods of time. Trots and canters should be kept to within a half mile at a time for a horse that is only ridden occasionally or on weekends.

If you have gotten on in a paddock or pasture and have

Competitive trail rides offer a challenging variation in everyday riding. The horse is judged over a measured course completed in a given time period. This horse is crossing the finish line in a 20 mile judged pleasure ride, and is being timed in by the official timer.

to open the gate to get out, you can learn to do this from horseback, provided that the gate has a suitable latch (one that can be opened and closed with one hand). If the gate fastens on the left, hold the reins in the left hand and position your horse so the latch is on your right and you are where you can reach it.

In this position, you can open the gate with your right hand. The horse's shoulder should be just to the left of the gate, so you can swing it open without hitting him. If your horse handles well, you should be able to open the gate and hold it while you ride through, turning around to the right when you get through the opening. Or, if you have to, you can let the gate swing open, and then turn and close it with your left hand. If the gate opens on the right you will have to use your left hand to open it, with the horse on the right side of the gate post.

Learning to open gates from horseback takes some practice, but once both you and the horse are accustomed to it, it should save much time for you. If your horse doesn't respond well to leg pressure, and won't move away from your leg, you will need to work on this before opening a gate will be easy for you. When he does learn this, opening gates will be good practice for this exercise and for teaching the horse to stand still, even when you have to lean to one side off balance.

You probably shouldn't try to open a gate from horseback if your horse gets excited easily and won't stand well, or if he has a tendency to rear, until you have practiced standing him quietly in front of the fence and gate for a while. Also practice getting on and off in front of or beside the gate so he doesn't want to turn around or move off.

If you get off to open the gate, take the reins over the horse's head before you try to open the gate, or if you have Western reins that aren't fastened together leave one hanging over the horse's neck and hold onto the other one. When you lead him through, make sure that you open the gate far enough so that it doesn't catch him as he goes through, and don't close it on his hocks.

It is very important to let your horse get "warmed up" at the beginning of a ride. Don't start right off at a trot or a canter, but walk the first five or ten minutes of each ride. This lets the saddle settle and lets the horse loosen up. It also helps prevent colic or founder if the horse has just eaten. Walking the first mile or two also helps cut down on the possibility of the horse wanting to kick up his heels when starting out.

Remember that you are training your horse every time you ride. You should keep this in mind and be careful of how you give signals and handle the horse.

As you ride, you will come across many variations in terrain and many natural obstacles. You should think about these obstacles before you are confronted with them.

Depending on where you live, you may come across hills when you ride cross-country. You should always lean well forward when climbing hills, to help keep the horse's balance and to keep a strain off his hind legs. The steeper the hill, the more you should lean forward. Unless the horse is in condition, don't let him run uphill, except for short hills with solid footing. When going downhill, try to maintain a fairly upright seat to keep in balance with the horse. Rising just slightly out of the saddle will help the horse to get his hind legs under him to go down the hill. As a general rule, don't go downhill any faster than a slow trot, as there is danger of falling. When going down a very steep hill or slide, try to keep the horse going in a straight line. He may "turn turtle" if you let him go down sideways.

One of most troublesome obstacles on the trail, for some people at least, is a creek. Many horses flatly refuse to cross a creek with a rider. Some are genuinely afraid of the water; others just don't want to go across and use it as an excuse to get out of work. Whichever the problem, you should teach the horse to go across anyway.

The first thing to do is to look the crossing over and decide whether it is safe or not. Try to find a spot where the banks of the creek are sloping and low. If you can't find one, and the banks are steep and high, you may be better off leading the horse across, unless you know from experience that he can and will cross safely.

In addition to how high the banks of the creek are, the footing across it is important. Usually you can tell by looking at it whether or not the ground is boggy. A creek with a gravelly bottom is usually solid, but very black soil or grayish clay is usually soft. Red clay may be sloppy, but usually has a solid base a few inches down. White sand is usually solid, but grayish sand may be *very* deep. If a normally willing horse balks at the footing, it may be best to take his word for it. Some horses seem to be able to sense soft ground, while others just plod merrily on through it.

When you've checked out the banks and the footing, don't forget to check what's on the other side of the creek. You don't want to cross where there are a lot of little overhanging trees or into a batch of briers or a big fallen tree. Sometimes you have to get down in the creek and walk up or down it a little to find a clear spot to come out. Avoid getting close to the big pools formed under trees on the creek bank, as they are often very deep and the footing around them may be soft.

As you ask the horse to cross a creek, be prepared for a jump. Many horses will jump anything short of a river, so don't be caught off guard and end up in the water. Lean forward, grab a piece of mane about halfway up the horse's neck, and use your other hand to steer. In a Western saddle, you might want to brace on the horn so it doesn't hit you in the stomach when you land from the jump. Give the horse plenty of rein by pushing your hand forward up his neck, but don't let your reins trail out so that they are too long. You may need short reins to turn the horse into the creek in case he tries to whirl away.

Let the horse take his time, and let him put his head down for a drink. Don't let him stop for too long, or walk up and down, however, as many horses like to lie down in a creek. Signs that he is about to lie down are pawing, pushing his nose around in the water, and generally hunching down. If you feel any of these, pull his head up and use your legs strongly.

If your reactions are too slow and he does lie down, the best thing to do is to get off and give him a swift kick in the rear. Yelling at him helps, too.

If you have to get off in the creek, or had to lead him into it in the first place, be careful when you lead him out. Try not to get directly in front of him as most horses will lunge up the bank quite suddenly. Hold the reins out near the end, keeping away from the horse, and climb the bank and let him come up beside you. Or, if you can move quickly enough, put your hand on his neck and walk out beside him.

If your horse balks at a creek, you may have to get a little rough with him. If he acts really afraid of the water, get off and try to coax him across. Get your hand wet and hold it up to his nose, to show him it's only water. Try taking some water and rubbing it on the horse's shoulders and legs. If you're riding with a friend, have him cross the creek first and see if your horse will follow. As a last resort, use the ends of the reins or a switch from a tree to "spank" him across.

If you don't want to get off the horse, and he balks, use your legs and the reins or a switch strongly. Let him take it one step at a time if necessary. If he's afraid of it enough to snort and blow, take your time and coax him. Otherwise he's putting you on, and you'll have to get after him. If the banks are shallow and the way is clear, getting a trotting start may help. Keep the reins short but not tight, and keep him from turning back. If he keeps turning and you can't stop him, try spinning him in a circle until he's dizzy and then head him for the creek. Sometimes just outlasting his patience is the only way to get a stubborn horse across. (Actually, I've never seen a person yet who could outlast a horse for stubbornness, but it's a nice thought, anyway.)

You may also come across a swamp or boggy place in your riding. Some wet areas are caused by run-off water collecting in low spots. These are usually solid and don't cause problems. Some bogs, however, are formed by underground springs or by a creek getting clogged by debris and water collecting over a long period of time. This creates wet ground for several feet down, and this type of mud can put a severe strain on a horse's legs. These spots are best avoided.

If you do come across a boggy spot, stop and look it over. Go around it if possible, unless you're sure it is just a puddle. If you must cross a bog, let the horse pick his own way, giving him plenty of rein so he can use his head and neck for balance. If the horse flounders in deep mud, stay on as long as he is moving ahead, but get off if he stops. Trying to dismount while he is struggling may cause him to fall. If he stops and doesn't move, don't worry. He is probably just resting, and will try to get out again when he is ready. In the unlikely event of his actually getting stuck so he can't get out, you may have to go for help. Take the saddle off and tie the bridle reins around the horse's neck so he can't trip on them. This way, if he should get out while you are away, he won't fall or roll on the saddle (which would break the tree, or frame) and he won't trip on the reins and break them if he runs home. Don't tie him up, even if there is a tree handy, as he will want to get away from the mud and may break the bridle reins in his efforts. If you have to get a tractor or other vehicle to pull the horse out of mud, make sure you bring plenty of rope along too. Don't use chains, and avoid tying ropes to the horse's legs, as they are easily injured. It is better to run the rope in a figure-eight pattern over his back and around either his chest or hindquarters.

Another obstacle you may come across is a bridge. Most horses will hesitate at crossing a strange bridge, and you can hardly blame them. They can sense that the structure is not truly solid, and it makes them nervous. Generally, if there is a crossing in the creek next to the bridge it is best to use that. If you do have to cross the bridge itself, look it over carefully first. If it is used by cars, you can assume that it is strong enough to hold the horse's weight, but if it is a foot bridge, it may not be. Check it for holes and loose boards as well. If necessary, find something to cover the holes (like an old board lying around). Unless you have crossed this bridge before, you should probably get off and lead the horse across it. Take it slowly and let him sniff it and take his time. Talk to him and coax him across. Try not to get directly in front of him as he may lunge across and knock you down or even off the bridge. Don't hold the reins too close to the bit; give him some head room so he doesn't feel confined. If you have an English saddle, run the stirrups up or at least cross them over the saddle so he doesn't catch them on the railing, if any. Don't ride two horses across a bridge side by side, although letting them follow head to tail may help a timid horse across.

Never cross a bridge faster than a walk, even if you have one of those nice horses that isn't afraid of anything. Be particularly careful if it is raining, or if the ground is wet, as bridges are slippery, especially wooden or asphalt ones. (Cinders aren't bad.)

When you come upon a field in your riding, don't just take off across it at a canter unless you have ridden there before and are familiar with it. Walk across or around a strange field, checking for holes (especially old fence post holes), old wire, and masses of briers or blackberry bushes.

Clumps of honeysuckle or weeds can hide ground hornets' nests or stumps. If you discover an old house, be on the lookout for the well since it may be hidden by weeds or even grown over. And a danger nowadays, particularly on land with "for sale" signs, is perc holes dug to test the ground for sewage construction possibilities. These holes are a foot square and at least three feet deep—treacherous.

Avoid crossing plowed, disced, or possibly seeded fields; ride around the edges instead. In addition to messing up the farmer's work, riding across a plowed field can pull a horse's tendons, particularly if he is out of shape. NEVER ride across a planted field, no matter how tempting the short cut or how dry the ground. You may find yourself strictly forbidden to use the property at all, even if it is your father's! Don't let your horse graze on wheat, or other planted field crops: they may make him sick.

If you have to ride along the highway, there are several safety precautions you should take. Broken bottles can cut a horse's coronet or fetlock, and the horse may stumble or slip on cans or bottles as well. Also, scraps of paper or piles of foul-smelling junk may make him shy. Watch your footing carefully and try to ride around the junk. If the shoulders of the road are grassy, remember that bottles may be hidden in the tall grass, and don't assume that it is easier on your horse's feet than the gravel. Unless the gravel is made of large, sharp rocks, you may be better off riding where you can see what you are walking on.

When you ride along the highway, pick a time of day when traffic is light; avoid rush hour. If your horse is afraid of trucks or school buses, avoid riding along the road on weekdays. Don't ride after the light has begun to fade in the evening, as it is difficult for motorists to see you in poor light, and the horse may tend to shy more easily at this time.

You should ride with the traffic (on the right side of

the highway) whenever possible. This may have its advantages, as most horses are more likely to shy from something heading for them, and if you ride with the traffic, approaching vehicles are on the other side of the road.

If you think that your horse may shy from a vehicle, move him as far away from the pavement as you can and stop him with his head facing it. Talk to him and pet him, and keep your reins short in case he tries to bolt. If he does bolt, or whirls to bolt, circle or spin him until the vehicle is past and he calms down. Don't punish a horse for shying at any kind of moving vehicle. It will only convince him that there is something bad about it after all. If you know that your horse shies at a certain kind of vehicle, such as a motorcycle, you may want to get off and hold him while one passes, although you may find it easier to control him if you stay on. Whether he will be calmer with you standing next to him will depend on the individual horse.

When you are riding in a group, remember that when one horse shies all of them will probably follow suit, so be prepared. Keep an eye on the horse ahead of you while you are riding. In a group, always ride with everyone on the same side of the highway and in single file.

Avoid riding on pavement itself; not only is it hard on the horse's legs, but it can be slippery, especially with a shod horse. It will also wear down the feet of an unshod horse rapidly.

When you have to cross the highway, wait until there is a clear enough space in the traffic to walk the horse across. Crossing at a faster gait may cause a fall. Some horses may be afraid to cross a blacktop road, so you may have to get off and lead one across. Always cross in single file, and make sure that you move all the way off the pavement by the time a car approaches.

One problem you will probably meet while riding on

the highway is dogs. Many will run out and at least pretend they are going to attack the horse. Most horses aren't really afraid of dogs, but one jumping out from the bushes may startle even a gentle horse into bolting or shying. When you approach a yard or group of houses, be on the alert. Take up a shorter rein, and tighten yourself in the saddle in case of a leap. Start talking to your horse and watch carefully. If you see a dog or dogs, stop your horse and wait, even if the dog is standing still or tied. Watch your horse's head; once he sees the dog, and pricks his ears in recognition, you can proceed. If a dog runs out at you, turn the horse to face it, and talk to him to quiet him down, if necessary. Once he sees what it is, he will probably settle down, and you can shout at the dog then. Give a few loud, commanding shouts of "Go home!" and it will probably run for cover. If the dog runs up behind the horse, try to keep him at a walk, and let him kick if he wants to. It may teach the dog a lesson and send him home. Since horses are quick to kick to protect themselves, there is little danger of a dog actually biting them. They are more of a nuisance than anything else.

Somewhere in your travels, particularly if you ride along the highway, you will probably find a nice gravel road. The temptation is great to canter or gallop down a road like this, but running on this type of road can cause severe leg or foot problems. A packed gravel road that is used by cars is as hard as, if not harder than, a paved road. Either walk the horse most of the way, keeping trotting and cantering down to short stretches, or use the softer shoulder as you would on the highway.

If you have to cross someone else's property on your rides, always ask for permission first. Be polite and thank them if they agree to let you ride there. If they don't sound too enthusiastic, thank them and find another way to ride;

don't push it. You may aggravate them to the point where they get their neighbors to deny you access too. When you do cross someone's land, be careful not to ride in the yard, and stay away from vehicles and animals so the horse doesn't accidentally damage anything. Stay off the crops and *always* leave gates the same way you found them. Never drop any litter, even a gum wrapper, anywhere but in proper trash cans. If the ground is muddy avoid riding on other people's property at all, as they may not like the deep hoofprints you leave.

What you do with your horse after you have finished riding can be as important as what you do while you ride. Improper care after a ride, especially a long or strenuous one, can lead to serious and permanent health problems for the horse.

You should always walk the horse for the last ten minutes before reaching home. This is to "bring him in cool." If your ride has worked the horse into a sweat and he is breathing hard and feels hot to the touch, at least on his chest and flanks, he is "hot." His respiration and heart rates are up, his blood is circulating rapidly, and his body temperature is elevated. His nostrils will be flaring and his flanks may be heaving as well. A horse in this condition may have a respiration rate of up to 100 beats a minute (from a normal of 12 to 15 per minute) and his heart rate may zoom from 36 or 40 to 80 or 100 beats per minute!

A horse stopped in this condition and given a quantity of cold water may founder immediately, or may even go into shock. Founder is the inflammation of the sensitive laminae (a lining in the interior of the hoof) of the front feet, caused by congestion of blood in the feet. It can be brought about by any condition that increases the circulation in the feet to the point where the blood pools rather than circulating back up the legs. Overworking or watering a hot horse can bring this on because when the horse drinks cold water his body temperature drops rapidly in the extremities. This causes a rapid slowdown of circulation in the legs. While the force of gravity and the horse's pounding heart send the blood down the legs rapidly, the slowed down circulatory system cannot pull it back up fast enough, and congestion, or founder, occurs. The symptoms are immediate lameness or soreness in one or both forefeet, heat in the affected foot, increased respiration, anxiety, and sweating in patches, especially on the neck and flanks.

If a horse is brought in hot and put away like that, he may founder even if he isn't watered. If he was ridden hard, putting him away without walking him around may cause his legs to swell ("stocking up"), stiffness, muscle cramps, or chills.

Walking a hot horse the last mile or two home will bring his respiration down slowly and allow his body temperature and heart rate to return to normal without complications. It will also allow tired muscles to relax slowly and restore proper circulation.

Sometimes it is impossible to cool the horse down on the trail, or he may still be hot after a ten minute walk. Some horses are too nervous to cool out well under saddle, and a horse in soft condition that is overworked may take longer than usual to cool. If the horse is still hot when you get home, you will have to walk him out either in hand or on a longe line. If he is wet and the weather is cold or windy, a sheet should be put over him until he dries out. Once the horse's respiration is down, he can be stopped for a few minutes now and then and then walked until he cools down. A few sips of water can be given every five minutes or so, but not if it is icy cold. It is probably wise to put only a little water in the bucket at a time as it may be very difficult to pull the horse's head out of a full bucket of water before he has had too much.

If you have taken a long ride, don't pull the saddle off

as soon as you dismount. Run the stirrups up if it's an English saddle and loosen the girth only one notch or one inch on a Western saddle. Then walk the horse around for a few minutes. Loosen the girth gradually and take the saddle off at least ten or fifteen minutes after you get home. This helps keep the horse's back from getting sore. As you ride the tight girth and your weight in the saddle slow the circulation of blood under the saddle. When the pressure of the saddle is released, the blood rushes back and congestion may occur under the skin. This causes the soft, tender welts known as "heat bumps." They may go away in a few hours, or may retain heat and make the hair fall out. When this happens the hair often grows in white as the pigment is damaged.

When you do take the saddle off, a dousing with cold water helps keep heat bumps from forming. Check the back for sores, hot spots, or lumps. Check the girth area carefully for tenderness or rubs. If you do find a rubbed place, apply a medicated salve after swabbing the area down with water or peroxide.

If your ride was over strenuous ground or if you have been jumping, you may want to rub down the legs. Some people wrap the front legs with "track bandages" for support after a hard ride, but unless you are an expert at this you may cause more problems than you solve. A bandage that is too tight can impair the circulation and can cause excess heat in the legs which can affect the tendons. If you feel the horse may have sore legs, or if he has heat in the tendon area (behind the cannon bones) you can apply a liniment. Use horse liniment only, and never bandage over liniment, as this will blister the skin.

In hot weather the horse will appreciate a hosing down or sponging. Wait until he is cool before applying cold water, however, and start sponging or hosing on the legs and work up. (Remember the body temperature.)

In the winter keep a wet horse out of the wind and put a light blanket (sheet) on him until he is cool. Avoid putting a heavy blanket on a hot or sweaty horse.

When the horse has cooled down thoroughly, he can either be put in a stall or turned out. Turning him out is preferable, as he can work any stiffness out as he grazes. If you put him in a stall, give him a bucket of clean, fresh water. Check him in an hour or so. If the ride was very strenuous, get him out and walk him around after about an hour. Some stocking up in the hind legs can be expected after a ride, but check him for founder if his front legs swell. Exercise him at a walk, and check for a pulse in his heels. If he is sore or has a pulse or heat, stand him in cold water, and reduce his grain ration at least by half. (A full stomach slows the circulation in the feet by drawing it to the digestive tract.) If the horse founders severely, call the veterinarian.

CHAPTER 6

Ring Work

A ring or some kind of enclosure to ride in is a great help to any horse owner, and practically a necessity for someone who is training a young horse or trying to ready one for a show. A ring doesn't have to be fancy, and it can vary from a 40 or 50 foot training pen to a 100 by 150 foot show ring. If you are lucky enough to have a large area and sufficient money and manpower, having both a small and a large ring is even better.

A ring is handy for several reasons. While it is true that you can ride a horse for years and never put him in a ring, it is practically impossible to put any advanced training on a horse without an arena, or at least a level area where you can make a circle. You must do some "schooling" on your horse some of the time, or he will become untrained, to put it mildly. A good rider schools his horse every minute he's on him, and the horse shows it in his obedient performance. But a lazy or untrained rider "just rides," and the horse shows that, too. Simply because a horse lets you get on and ride him, doesn't mean he's trained. The difference between a trained horse and an untrained one is extraordinary.

You may be the kind of rider who looks at his friend's horses and says to himself, "How come my horse won't do all of those things? What's the magic formula that makes their horses jump into a canter from a walk, always take the correct lead, keep a nice even trot on a loose rein, and drop back to a walk without even trying?" If your horse is so bad that you feel like this, you must not be riding right! If you are having problems with your horse, or if he just goes along his merry way without really paying much attention to your signals, you need to start changing some of your riding habits. First of all, do you do all of your riding on trails? If so, you should start spending some time riding in a ring or field. You can either make a makeshift ring of hay bales (or something else solid enough for the horse to see easily) or hunt around until you find a field with natural boundaries (trees or a fence) on at least two sides.

The idea of using a ring for training is that it makes the horse work in a circle. This does several things for the horse. It makes him bend laterally and become supple, so that he can turn well and become quick on his feet. It gives him a place to work where he doesn't always have to be looking for his footing and worrying what's around the next bend, so he can concentrate better on your signals. It keeps him from wanting to stretch out and run because he soon realizes that he doesn't get anywhere running around in circles. (This is especially good for a horse that tends to want to run away.)

In short, working in a ring is so uninteresting that the horse pays more attention to his rider. While this is an advantage in some respects, the rider should keep this in mind and not overdo the ring work. A horse will get bored quickly by going around in circles, and if he is kept at it day after day, he will probably get "sour," which means he goes with an "I hate everybody" attitude, head down, ears back, tail wringing. I know it seems like a contradiction to say "Ride in the ring, it's important," and then say, "Don't ride in the ring very much, it's bad for the horse." But the difference lies in how much you ride in the ring. Use it enough to get the horse working as you want him to, but don't overdo it. Don't ride in the ring every day; spend two out of every five riding days on the trail, for instance. Don't ride in the ring for more than about an hour at a time without a break outside, even if it's just a turn or two around the field or up and down the road. Don't work in the ring past the point where the horse is working well and is beginning to tire.

When you ride in a ring (from now on, when I say ring, I mean any enclosed place or circular track) spend enough time "on the rail," or close to the fence, to get the horse so he will keep out of the center without your having to hold him there. Do this by riding with a strong outside rein and strong inside leg when the horse tries to cut in. Once he is used to working on the rail, you can vary this work by cutting across the middle, making figure eights, doubling back on the rail, etc. You can practice making smaller and smaller circles, stopping, backing, etc. in the ring. Using the fence as a visual barrier may help teach the horse to stop better.

There are several things about the routine of a ring that may cause problems. The horse will quickly learn where the gate is and will want to stop there, especially if you always get on and off, or stop, near the gate. Since you can't move the gate around, you should either lead him into the ring and get on at varying spots, or change the place where you stop work from time to time. Don't always go to the center of the ring to stop, however, or your horse will head for the center constantly.

If the horse does balk at passing the gate or tries to head for it all the time, he will have to be convinced that he can't do this. First try to decide if boredom is his problem. You may be working him in the ring too much. Or you may be letting him stop at the gate more often than you realize, or letting him slow down near it. When you go around the ring, pay attention and start to correct him just before he starts for the gate. You may want to steer him out away from the fence past the gate for a while, or even work at the other end of the ring for a time. As you near the gate, shorten the inside rein and start using strong leg pressure on the side near the gate. Try to keep the horse at the same speed all the way around the ring, even past the gate.

Some horses brace their necks against the bit and bulldoze right into the gate. If this happens, don't just give up and let the horse stand there. This is rewarding him for running to the gate. When your horse runs to the gate and stops at it, "murder" him. Punish him as long as he is standing there, by kicking him or smacking him with a crop, and stop punishing when he moves away, even if it is only a few steps. Pull the horse's head away from the gate if it helps, but don't yank him in the mouth. If the horse tends to rear, you may be better off not pulling on his mouth at all, but just kicking him. Since he can't walk over the gate, he will have to move off alongside the fence. If your horse is not the excitable type, using the crop against the side of his neck next to the gate may help turn him away from it. Generally if you are nasty enough with your crop and/or heels any horse will move away from the gate simply because he cannot go through it. (This doesn't work with a makeshift fence!) As a last resort, you can get off and lead him away from the gate.

The best remedy, of course, is to keep the horse from running to the gate in the first place. Sometimes it is easier

than you think it will be. You must keep in mind that
while you can't always stop a horse, you can turn him.
The secret to this is called the "double," and while it is
usually considered a "Western" training trick, I find it useful on all kinds of horses.

The "double" turns the horse around in his tracks, by
turning his head so far around that he has to turn or fall
down. The double is used at a walk, and I have never yet
had a horse fall down with me while doing this. At faster
gaits than a walk, the turn is done a little more gradually.

To double a horse, take one rein in each hand. Then
reach up and hold one rein as close to the bit as you can,
and pull the horse's head around toward your knee. Lean
toward the turn, and use the opposite leg strongly. This
should spin the horse around in his tracks, or at least
change his direction drastically.

With a horse that is trying to take you to the gate, the
time to double him is just as he starts for the gate. Double
him around so he is facing the opposite direction, and he
will stop automatically. If you have let him get too close
to the gate, or are going too fast to double, you can pull
him to the side away from the gate as hard as you can and
use the leg toward the gate strongly to keep him going past
it. Don't leg him into the fence from a distance or he may
try to jump it. If you have his head turned far enough to
one side he will have to follow the fence.

You can use the double anywhere and anytime your
horse refuses to stop or to turn. You can use it with any
type of bit or hackamore. It works especially well with a
bosal (rawhide hackamore). You can even use the double
on a horse that rears, if you catch the horse before he gets
up very high. If the horse fights turning, you can spin him
around a few times with the double. A horse can't rear
when he's spinning.

If you use the double very often (and you may have to

The horse gets "doubled" when he refuses to stop or turn. The rider pulls his head around to his knee and makes the horse turn about. This young horse gets upset at this manuever, and riders are advised to use this technique sparingly. An older, spoiled horse, especially one of quiet temperament, may benefit greatly by this exercise if it is done properly.

for a while with a stubborn horse), be sure to turn him equally in both directions, or you will end up with a horse that will turn only one way.

It is very important to ride both ways of a ring or circle equally; otherwise you will develop a one-sided horse. When a horse works in a circle he uses the muscles on one side more than the other. If you ride him more in one direction than the other, he will become stronger on one side than the other, and he will resist being ridden on his "soft" side.

You can tell if your horse is one-sided by riding a circle. Does he feel more awkward or stiff going one way than the other at the trot? Does he feel smooth on one diagonal but rough on the other? Does he take one lead more readily than the other? If he feels different going in one direction, the smooth side is his "good" side. To correct the problem, you will have to work him more on his bad side than you do on the good, until both sides are equally smooth. Pay attention to how much you work in each direction. If you walk three times around to the right, then sometime during that ride you should walk three times to the left. If you are correcting a one-sided problem, you might want to work twice as long on the poor side. Equal work means equal time at the same speed, with some variation. Working at a canter puts more stress on the horse than the same amount of work at an ordinary trot, for instance. An extended trot, however, creates more stress than a slow canter.

In addition to varying the spot where you begin work each day, you should change the place where you get off from time to time. Many horses will try to run into the middle of the ring, because their riders make a habit of stopping and dismounting there. This is particularly common in horses that have been shown a lot. The horse that

Most horses are at least somewhat one-sided. This filly is resisting the turn to the right and gets "strung out."

Turning to the left, however, she bends more readily and keeps her legs under her. More work on the right side will limber her up and help her to turn equally well in both directions.

tries to end the work period early by heading for the "line up" can be very difficult to keep on the rail. This habit can be prevented by making a practice of dismounting on the rail at least half the time, somewhere away from the gate.

For the horse that already has the habit of trying to cut into the center, ride close to the fence and use a strong outside rein and inside leg pressure. Use the crop on the inside of his neck, if necessary. Ride this way only as much as it takes to keep the horse near the fence, as you may have to pull his head out of alignment, and this way of moving might become a habit also. Some horses go around the ring with their noses practically hanging over the fence as a result of being held out to the rail too strongly. Try to use more leg pressure than rein in order to keep the horse from doing this.

When you reverse direction in the ring, turning the horse toward the fence may help keep him from heading for the middle of the ring.

If you ride Western and work in a ring, you will probably try either racing patterns or reining work at some time. Riders who plan to show in pattern classes should learn the pattern well at home and make sure the horse can do it well before trying to enter a show. This does not mean that you should practice the patterns every time you ride, or do them over and over again. Some horses learn patterns very easily and will begin to anticipate the movements in them if they are practiced too much. Teach the horse each movement in the pattern correctly, and learn the pattern so you can do it without getting off course. Then you can practice the pattern as much as your horse will tolerate without becoming bored or trying to take shortcuts in the pattern. Working with the ears back, wringing the tail, and generally acting sluggish are signs of boredom. Changing leads too soon or not at all, zig-zagging before a turn, and slowing down before a stop is requested are some of the signs of anticipating the pattern.

Once you have figured out the pattern in your head, start your horse on it at a walk. (This goes for racing patterns too.) Work the pattern, or do it in parts, if necessary, for a few repetitions two or three times a week until he will go through the whole pattern at a walk smoothly, without your having to kick him or pull him around a turn. In any pattern, expect the horse to make smooth, rounded turns, with his head slightly toward the direction of the turn, and smooth, straight stops. Working the pattern at a walk will help both you and the horse to learn it. If the horse can't do the pattern well at a walk, he shouldn't be expected to do it at a faster gait.

When the horse can do the pattern at a walk, do it at a jog or trot. (English horses can do patterns, too; they're good practice for control and balance.) By this time the horse may already be anticipating the movements, so vary things a little. Learn several simple patterns and do parts of them together, change the size of the pattern, run it backwards, or do part one day and the rest the next. Try practicing the individual maneuvers in a pattern for a week or so. You can also move the place of the pattern work, which will give the horse new visual boundaries to adjust to. Use anything you can think of to keep the horse from getting bored and lazy.

Don't start to canter or lope a pattern until the horse can do the movements correctly at a trot. You may be able to do some of the maneuvers at a canter while working on the tough ones at a slower speed, however. When you do begin to canter the pattern, start by doing individual movements and work up to cantering the entire pattern. If your horse tends to get excited, you may want to vary the speed within the pattern for a while. If the horse gets very upset about cantering the pattern, continue working at a walk and trot until he settles down.

If the horse gets very used to a pattern and tries to take shortcuts even though you don't work the pattern very often, you may want to stop doing patterns at all for a month or so at a time. For the horse that never seems to learn the pattern at all, try repeating just one part of it over and over to see if that helps. Some horses are slow learners.

One of the problems encountered with racing patterns is the horse that gets too "hot" and wants to run all the time. He may get so excited that he will goof up a course in his hurry to get through it. Many horses that are raced get so excited at the beginning that they are almost impossible to control at the starting line. Others get so they refuse to enter the ring. Some get in the habit of slacking off before the finish line because they know they're going to stop. The best solution to these problems is to lessen your racing work. Walk the patterns at least as often as you run them. Try running the patterns outside the ring part of the time. Changing the place of the starting and finishing lines may also help. As for the horse that won't enter the ring, lead him in part of the time, and try to cut down on the time spent racing in the ring.

CHAPTER 7

Jumping

Sooner or later most English riders decide to try jumping, and many Western riders enjoy hopping over a log on the trail occasionally. Jumping is fun and very exhilarating, and dangerous only when done recklessly or over jumps too difficult for the horse and/or rider's ability and training.

Jumping is fun for the horse, too, if he is not overtaxed and if the rider does not interfere with his natural movements over the jump. If you watch a horse jumping, or even look at some pictures of jumping horses, you will notice that the horse stretches his head and neck out and arches his back when he jumps. This extension and arching of the back increase with the height and width of the jump.

Jumping is a difficult feat for the horse because it requires him to propel himself into the air in an arc and then land on both front feet at the same time. It takes strength, conditioning, and balance for a horse to do this well, and to jump without discomfort or pain. While the horse is in the air he is balanced somewhat precariously, and his landing can be upset by a sudden shift in balance by the rider.

Thus the rider must interfere with the horse as little as possible while he is jumping. This mainly involves giving the horse enough rein to extend his head and neck as much as he needs to without restraint. It is also important to follow through with your body so that your weight does not shift back onto the horse's spine during the jump or while landing. This is not too important when jumping small jumps, but as the height increases so does the danger of upsetting the horse and making him fall.

If you have tried to jump your horse, but he doesn't seem to jump well, or refuses to jump, some evaluation is needed. While most horses can jump low jumps (2 or 3 feet) quite well, some horses do not have the conformation to be good jumpers. Short, thick necks, straight shoulders and pasterns, or very light, weak hindquarters are some of the conformation faults that make it hard for a horse to jump well. If your horse resists jumping, try to watch someone else jump him or watch him jump without a rider (on a longe line, perhaps). If he jumps awkwardly even without a rider, he may just not be built for it.

A horse must have strong, sound feet and legs and a strong back to be able to jump comfortably. Being uncomfortable for one reason or another is probably the most common reason for a horse to be reluctant to jump. Horses with poor feet, especially those which have been foundered, may resist jumping because the impact hurts their feet. Horses with very small feet in relation to their size may also have this problem. A horse with a very short back and neck may have difficulty arching his back well enough to jump, and may get sore muscles from trying to accomplish this. If a horse resists jumping or will only jump very low jumps, it might be worthwhile to have a veterinarian check him over for foot, leg, or back problems.

If the horse's problem is not physical you will have to

assume either that you are the cause of his reluctance to jump or, in the case of a new horse, that a previous owner caused him to dislike or fear jumping. This is a time for honest self-evaluation. Admitting that you may be causing the problem may be a sizable step in curing the dislike the horse has for jumping. Consider how good a rider you are in general. If your seat is not secure enough for you to canter and gallop cross-country (including over rough ground and around turns) without losing your balance or pulling on your horse's mouth, you should put off jumping until you are more experienced, or at least confine your jumping efforts to trotting over low jumps. You must be able to ride without depending on your hands to help you keep your balance, so that you don't accidentally pull your horse's mouth over a jump. If your horse is *very* dependable about jumping, you may be able to hold onto his mane until you can balance well enough.

If your control of your horse on the flat is poor or inadequate, even at times, you should improve this before you try jumping. If the horse can get away with things in your day-to-day riding, such as running to the gate, you will probably not be able to keep him from running out around a jump if he wants to. You should practice stopping and turning at all gaits before you decide to start jumping. Practice riding with your reins short, but without contact on the horse's mouth. The reins should have little or no slack in them, and your hands will have to move back and forth with the motion of the horse's head. With your hands in this position you can put contact on the horse's mouth without having to move your hands back very far, which is helpful when the horse lands from a jump and still has his head fairly high.

Learning to ride in "jump position" will also help you develop a good seat for jumping. It helps keep you from thumping the horse's back during a jump. If you ride with your stirrups fairly long, shorten them until the bottom of the stirrup hits your ankle bone when your legs are hanging straight. Then practice standing in your stirrups and leaning forward over the horse's neck. You should be balanced over your feet with your seat just clearing the saddle. Your heels should be well down and you should be able to keep your balance even if you let go with your hands. It is a good idea to practice this position until you can hold it for ten or twelve strides at all gaits without using your hands.

This is the position you will use during jumping, and you should use it up to and after jumps until you have learned to judge when the horse will take off and land. This will help prevent you from "getting left behind," which means getting left sitting on the saddle as the horse goes over the jump, instead of being balanced over the withers.

No matter how experienced a jumper your horse is, if you have never jumped before you should start with jumps only one and one-half to two feet high, and should jump from a trot. This will give you more control and help you learn to judge the horse's take-off point.

Your jumps don't have to be elaborate, but they should be at least 10 feet wide and solid-looking to the horse. He should be able to see the top line clearly. It helps to have some kind of uprights (standards) on the ends of the jumps. You should try to have at least two jumps set up at a time if you are planning to train the horse to jump in shows, or he will not be used to jumping courses of several jumps and he will not make a smooth, even performance over a number of jumps in the show ring.

Jumps can be made of many things, although there are some things they should *not* be made of. *Never* jump over

The rider should practice riding in "jump position" before trying to learn to jump. Stand in the stirrups and lean forward, with the hands forward. There is nothing wrong with holding onto the mane or the neck, at least at first, and if your horse jumps reliably you may never need to learn to jump without holding on. Of course, show jumping will require more skill and finesse than doing it just for fun.

any kind of wire fence or obstacle. For one thing, the horse probably can't see it, and it would be disastrous if he got caught in it. Avoid things that would splinter or break if hit by the horse or stepped on (thin plywood, for instance). Until you and your horse are both experienced, don't make jumps that are really solid and unbreakable, because of the possibility of your falling on them if the horse refuses. Bales of hay or straw, tires propped against a pole, barrels, etc., all make good jumps. Poles are very popular and handy because you can add more to make a jump higher or cross them. Do not make a high jump with just one pole because the horse has trouble judging how high the jump is with a thin top line and no bottom line. Try to make jumps that have definite outlines that don't blend into the background. Jumps can be vertical (such as a pole jump) or spread (with depth, like a barrel or chicken coop). As spread fences are more difficult, you should start a horse on simple verticals and add spreads later in training.

Perhaps the most important thing to remember about jumping is that it is hard on the horse and can be boring too. Therefore it is wise not to overdo it. Keep the height low and the pace slow until the horse is conditioned to jumping. Jump him over one height until he is trotting and cantering over it willingly and smoothly before you try higher jumps. Raise the jumps only three to six inches at a time.

Don't jump your horse every day. At first, jump only once or twice a week, and only six or eight jumps a day. When the horse has been jumping for six months or so, you can raise him to 10 or 12 jumps in a day, if he will tolerate it. Remember that as the height goes up the work becomes harder.

Try to put some variety in your horse's jumping, once he has learned to jump willingly. Some horses seem to be willing to jump at any time, but others get bored easily. Change the course around from time to time, putting it in different places or varying the order of the jumps. Keep the jumps about sixteen feet or farther apart. If your horse always has to put in an extra little stride before each jump, space them a little farther apart. You can also vary the height within a course, but not by more than three to six inches.

Jump on smooth, level ground until the horse is experienced, since uneven footing will make it more difficult for him to judge his takeoffs, and he may hurt himself working on rough ground. Later, when the horse is in condition, you can put the jumps on a slight hill or in a rolling field, to add variety and prepare the horse for hunting, if desired. Don't jump on wet grass or in mud, as the horse may slip on the takeoff and hurt himself. Don't jump on frozen ground as it is very hard and may be slippery.

You should not consider jumping a horse until he is at least four years old. Horses do not mature until they are five, and jumping a young horse may do permanent damage to his legs. Overworking a young horse may make him break down (become unsound in legs or back) at an early age. A healthy horse may be ridden well into his twenties, but one that has been worked too hard when young may have only 10 or 12 useful years.

If your horse is normally a willing jumper but becomes slow and uninterested, or starts trying to run out or refuse, try giving him a break by not jumping him at all for a few weeks. Change his work schedule around to give him something new to do, and when you do start jumping again, start with the jumps a little lower than when you left off. Also try cutting down on the number of jumps per ride, or the number of jumping days per week.

When your horse consistently refuses a jump, try lowering the height, even if you have to make it very small. If it is very low to start with, try taking it at a different pace (trot if you have been cantering). Try giving the horse more of an approach to it, or if you have been giving him a long one, try starting closer to the jump. Make sure you are not holding him too tightly, and make sure you are encouraging him to go over the jump, not bracing against him to keep from falling off should he stop. Many times a rider will stiffen up and brace to make sure he can stay on, and this actually asks the horse to stop by working against him. If the horse wants to stop anyway, this gives him an excuse to. The saying, "Throw your heart over the fence" is worth thinking about: you may fall off more often, but your horse will stop refusing as often.

Check to make sure you aren't pulling on the horse's mouth over the jump, or otherwise hurting him. Grab

Over the jump the most important thing is to give the horse enough head and to stay off his back. This rider braces on the neck so she doesn't fall back and jerk the mouth. The horse stretches his neck out over even low jumps, and it is easy to catch him in the mouth. Moving the hands forward up the neck enables the rider to give the horse plenty of rein without losing control by letting the reins slide through the hands.

A more advanced rider follows the horse's head with the hands and does not use the neck for support. Contact can be maintained this way, and the rider has more control, but if the rider has trouble keeping his balance he should grab mane and save the horse's mouth.

mane and keep a loose rein over a few jumps, and stay up in jump position for several strides before and after each jump for a while. If the horse becomes more willing after a few jumps like this, it should tell you something. If you wear spurs, make sure you aren't jabbing the horse in the sides over the jumps.

If giving strong leg signals into a jump doesn't get the horse to go over, and if you are certain that the horse is sound and that you aren't doing anything to cause the problem, you may want to try using a crop. Remember, however, that using a crop may often make the horse more certain that jumping is a bad thing and it may make him worse instead of better. Use your crop judiciously. Give the horse a chance to go over the jump for you with body and leg aids. If he starts to refuse the fence, use the crop sharply once or twice behind the girth. If the horse does jump, reward him immediately following the landing by either quitting for the day or by giving him a rest before jumping again that day. If the horse stops anyway, you may want to give him *one* hard crack behind the girth as a punishment, then take him at the jump again immediately. You can back him away from the jump if he backs well, to keep his mind on the jump. Do not hit the horse anywhere but behind the girth—*never* on the head. Absolutely do *not* yank the horse in the mouth for refusing, since he will think you are punishing him for not stopping fast enough—which is very confusing. In addition, the pain caused by this will linger for several minutes, making him even less likely to want to jump again.

The horse that chronically runs out may be cured by putting long, high wings on each side of the jump, or by putting one end of the jump up against a fence and a wing on the other side. Lower the jumps for a time and follow the guidelines set up for a refusal to jump, trying to eliminate any reasons why the horse might not want to jump. You may find it necessary to backtrack in the horse's training for a while and jump some low jumps at a trot until the horse regains his confidence. Most horses have a favorite side to run out to. This is often the horse's "good" side, and a one-sided horse may not show his stiffness on one side in any other situation. Spend some time hacking in circles to build up the turning ability of the horse to the opposite side than the one he runs out to. Once you have figured out which side the horse generally heads for, ride with strong leg pressure on that side and a strong rein on the other side. Reward the horse for going over a jump by using your voice and giving him a short rest. Resist the temptation to yank the horse into the jump as he may trip over the standard and further disenchant himself with jumping.

Horses refuse to jump because (a) it hurts them; (b) they are afraid of the jump; or (c) they know they can get away with it. Try to determine which reason or reasons your horse has for refusing before you try to correct the problem. Take into account your individual horse's temperament and ability. Take things slowly and give the horse a chance to develop the proper muscles and coordination before expecting him to jump too high or too often. If your horse is the spooky type, keep him on plain jumps until he is reliable and calm before adding new or different jumps.

Don't try to show your horse in a jumping class until you know that he can and will smoothly and calmly jump all of the kinds of jumps used in a show at the same heights used. School him at home, show off in a show. If you discover that he wasn't ready after all and he refuses or runs out in the ring, don't lose your temper and whip him. This may give him a permanent fear of jumping in a show ring, not to mention making a fool of you. Take your defeat gamely and go home with the aim of working until he is ready. If it is the first show he has ever jumped in, don't enter him in more than one or two jumping classes or you may tire him out and sour him on show-ring jumping.

If the horse falls while jumping, or on the approach to a jump, first let him get up and stand for a few minutes. Check him for injury by leading him first at a walk, then at a slow trot. If he seems all right you can get on and ride him slowly for a few minutes. Then lower the jump and take him over it once to help keep him from developing a fear of jumping. It is then usually best to stop riding for the day, as a fall will often pull muscles and cause soreness.

Do not jump a horse that has been injured or lame until you are positive he is fully recovered. It is best to get the veterinarian's advice, as jumping could reinjure the horse or make him worse. When you do begin to jump again, keep the number and height of the jumps low at first, until the horse is built up again.

It is usually a good idea to rub a horse's legs down with liniment after a jumping session and especially after a show. You could bandage the horse's legs for support, if you know how to properly. Do not apply both liniment and bandages as this will blister the horse's legs. Bandaging is usually better if the horse is to be kept stalled; liniment if he is to be turned out. Rub the horse's legs well before bandaging. Use a hard upward motion and a gentle downward rub, to encourage circulation in the legs below the knees. Wrap the front legs from just below the knees to just above the fetlock joint, or apply liniment to the tendon area.

CHAPTER 8

Problems Under Saddle

The person who doesn't have problems with his horse under saddle at some time or another probably doesn't ride him much—or at all! Because horses are individuals and are subject to good and bad moods, and because riders seldom have the presence of mind and the patience to always give the right signal at the right time, most horses develop bad habits from time to time. One of the challenges of riding is to try to keep these habits from forming, and to correct them once they are noticed.

A common problem is the horse that doesn't stop well, throws his head up on stops, or doesn't stop at all. This is one of those problems that is usually caused by the rider. If you don't give the horse enough warning that you are going to stop, don't give him time to stop properly, give poor signals to stop such as hauling back on the mouth with no leg or body aids, or don't reward the horse for stopping, he will eventually get so he either ignores your signals or makes a jerky, uncomfortable stop.

When you want your horse to stop, you should plan ahead before getting to the place where you want to start

127

slowing down. You must warn the horse that he is about to stop and then give him an opportunity to get ready by drawing his hind legs up under his body. You can give the warning signal in one of two ways, or you can combine the two, whichever works best on your horse. One way is to give a "tap" on the reins several strides before the actual stopping signal, which is a pull and release on the reins or freezing the hand, combined with a bracing of the back and a sitting down in the saddle motion of the seat. This can be accompanied also by the voice command, "Ho!" The other way is to warn the horse by using light leg pressure combined with light hand pressure to keep

Stopping on the forehand. The horse seems to be going downhill with his nose to the ground. The head position here is good, but the horse's forehand is lower than his hindquarters.

This is better, although still not perfect. The horse is stopping more or less level, but with the head too high. This filly had only been ridden for about a month when this picture was taken, and she's just learning.

the horse from speeding up, followed by the bracing of the back and sitting down aid of the seat.

If you try this signaling method on your horse (either English or Western), you will probably notice that his hindquarters seem to drop down a little when he stops, which is good. This means that he is drawing the hind legs under his body. If he feels like he's going downhill and you're going to fly over his head when he stops, it means that he is stopping on his forehand instead of being balanced.

You have probably heard the term "going on the forehand" many times if you go to shows. This is a common term that is apparently not understood by most amateur riders. Being "on the forehand" means that the horse is working with most of his weight on his front legs instead of more or less evenly distributed between front and rear legs.

When a horse is standing still, he naturally carries about two-thirds of his weight on his front legs. As soon as he begins to move, his center of gravity shifts and, as he uses his hind legs to propel him forward, his weight should shift to become evenly distributed. Most horses will balance naturally when loose, although horses with poor conformation may have to work on the forehand naturally to compensate for their structure. Horses with certain unsoundnesses of the legs or injuries may also redistribute their weight in abnormal ways in order to adjust to their problems. Watch your horse at play in the field or on the longe line to see whether he uses his hindquarters strongly to start, stop, and turn, or whether he carries his head down and works mostly with his front end. Look to see if he strides as fully with his hind legs as he does with the front. A horse that is naturally front-ended may be impossible to balance correctly when ridden. If your riding demands are light, this may not matter, but if you plan to show, event, hunt, or do competitive trail riding, you may need a more well-balanced horse.

When you ride, you can tell when your horse is on the forehand since he will feel like he is going downhill all the time. His head will usually be low, although a high head carriage does not necessarily mean that the horse is well balanced. A horse that is too heavy on the forehand will find it more difficult to take a canter from a walk, to stop from a canter without trotting, and to change leads at a canter, for instance.

When you watch a horse being ridden, you can tell if he is balanced by watching his legs. A balanced horse takes even strides with all four legs. In each stride he reaches up with his hind legs to the print left by the front feet. If the horse takes large steps with the front feet but small ones with the hind, he is too heavy on the forehand. His front legs are taking more than their share of the shock of movement, and the shock comes up the legs to the saddle and to you, making his gaits more jarring. The horse also loses much agility by being on the forehand.

Being able to recognize a horse that is on the forehand is the first step toward correcting this problem. Since some horses are naturally unbalanced, it may be impossible to correct their problem completely, but getting them to adjust their balance back to a natural level will be a noticeable improvement.

Basically, the solution to the problem of going on the forehand is to encourage the horse to use his hindquarters more. Riders sit just behind the withers because it is the strongest part of the horse's back. However, some horses seem to shift their weight forward onto their shoulders when ridden, possibly as a way of compensating for weakness in the back or hindquarters. In addition, most riders tend to give all or most of their signals to the horse's front end by using their hands for all the signals and neglecting leg and body aids. Many riders use their leg on the horse's shoulder to turn him, which is another way of encouraging him to use the forehand too much. Some even use the crop or reins on the horse's shoulder to get him to go, which is even worse. Since the horse is naturally inclined to throw his weight forward onto his shoulders, this type of riding gives him an excuse to get in the habit of dragging himself around by his forehand and letting his hindquarters become weak and undeveloped. Then the rider wonders why he can't get over a two and one-half foot jump!

Turning, heavy on the forehand. The horse seems to be spiraling towards the ground in front.

Turning, getting lighter. The filly's hindquarters are coming under her and she is learning to turn in a more balanced manner. Practicing small circles, keeping the horse's nose to the inside of the circle, helps.

The first step in correcting the problem is teaching the horse to respond to leg aids, and to learn to use your legs when you ride. If your horse will already do a turn on the forehand correctly (by moving away from the pressure of your leg and not depending on you to pull his head around) you may only need to start using your legs more while you ride. Instead of just letting your horse loaf along, try pushing him with alternating legs to get him to walk briskly, etc. If the horse tries to increase his speed too much, use the reins lightly to rate him. This will encourage the horse to take bigger steps with his hind legs, bringing them up under him and balancing him. This should raise his head slightly and put more spring in his step. Practice this for short periods until the horse is responding to it, and then increase the time when you do it until the horse will take over and do it himself.

Try to avoid hanging on the horse's mouth all the time. Use a give-and-take pressure on the mouth when necessary to rate his speed, since this rewards him for slowing down. At the same time, don't nag the horse with your legs all the time. Pay attention to him and use your legs only when he slacks off and shuffles along. When he is moving briskly with a lively step reward him by relaxing your leg pressure and let him enjoy being balanced and alert. Encourage your horse to keep an even speed around curves and turns, using your outside leg on curves to get the horse to push with his hindlegs through the turn.

If your horse doesn't respond to leg aids or doesn't know them, you need to teach him to obey them. There are several ways of doing this, and different ways work better on different horses. How well your horse responds probably depends a lot on how sensitive he is, in addition to his background.

The method I use to teach the horse leg aids seems to

work quickly on most horses, even those that have learned to ignore leg signals. Standing beside your horse with the reins in the hand closest to his head, press on his side about where your leg would be if you were mounted. Use a short stick or the end of your crop if your horse doesn't respond to your fingers poking him. If the horse tries to step forward, let him take one or two steps. As soon as he moves, stop pressing to reward him. Most horses will react to this pressure by taking a step away from you with the hindquarters, which is actually what you want. If he seems reluctant to move at all, turn his head toward you to give him the idea. When the horse does move, even one step, reward him by releasing the pressure, wait a moment, and then repeat the procedure. When he has made a 180 degree turn in one direction, walk him around a few times and then repeat the procedure in the other direction. Practice this until the horse will move from only a slight touch, keeping the sessions no longer than about 15 minutes at a time. The horse should learn this in a day or two. Since he may learn to anticipate your signals and begin turning as soon as you move to his side, spend about twice as much time just brushing him or running your hands down his sides while he is standing, so he learns to wait for a command to move away.

In a few days your horse should learn to move away from just a light pressure from your fingers. This will have taught him to move away from pressure on his side, and it will come in handy when you need to position him in hand, such as in lining up to a fence for mounting.

Once the horse will do a turn on the forehand (what you just taught him) in hand, get on and try it mounted. While he is standing still, press your leg against his side while you pull his head *slightly* to the side you are pressing on. If he tries to move forward when you squeeze, try standing him in front of a fence so he cannot move. Release the leg pressure the instant the horse takes a step away from it. At first be satisfied with only one step. When he has moved to one side, walk him around for a while and do it the other way. Later, when he has learned to respond well, you can progress to complete turns.

Once the horse has learned to do a turn on the forehand well, stop practicing it and go on to other things. Too much practicing of this will get the horse so he will turn away from your leg when you ask him to stop.

When the horse has begun to learn the turn on the forehand, he should automatically become more responsive to your legs when moving. If you have had problems getting your horse to respond to leg aids, make sure you are not using your reins to give conflicting signals, and make sure you reward the horse for obedience to your legs by releasing the pressure at the right time. Once you get the horse into a gait, don't keep rating his speed down for a while, until he becomes more responsive. One of the things that can cause a horse to become sluggish is having the rider constantly picking at his mouth to slow him down. The horse gets the feeling that there is no point in obeying the leg aids because the rider is going to pull him down as soon as he speeds up. Let him get settled in a gait before slowing him down, and then try letting him go a little faster in his gaits than you were before. You may have been trying to impose a speed on him that is slower than it is comfortable for him to maintain. This may also cause him to become too heavy on the forehand.

Another thing that causes problems with horses is nagging with the legs. The difference between nagging and pushing the horse with your legs to achieve balance is *timing*. Pushing your horse up consists of using alternating leg pressures which stop for a stride or two when the horse responds (reward) and resume if he begins to lag. Nagging with the legs means kicking more or less constantly, or at least without timing the release to the movement of the horse. Some horses rebel against too much leg pressure more quickly than others. Some become sluggish, some nervous wrecks. It is easy to get into the vicious cycle of nagging the horse. You kick him, he doesn't respond, or at least not fast enough to suit you, so you kick him again. Then it seems the more you kick, the slower he goes. Pretty soon you get tired of kicking so you start in with the crop. Sometimes this works if the horse is fairly sensitive, but sometimes it just gives you a horse that won't go no matter what you do. This is because he feels that if you hit him no matter what he does (or so it seems to him) that he might just as well stand still: at least, this gets him out of work.

Sound familiar? The solution, believe it or not, is quite simple, at least in most cases. The idea is to reward the horse for the slightest obedience. This will probably take a good hour or so of absolute patience from the rider for the first day or two, but it will be well worth it. It is the only method I know of that is truly effective and does not involve trying to force the horse to obey (which doesn't work anyway), and it doesn't make the horse nervous or afraid of being ridden.

Lead the horse into the ring or out into the field to a spot where he used to perform willingly. There is no point in doing this where he normally balks anyway or where he naturally wouldn't want to go, such as in front of the barn or gate. Turn the horse toward home and get on. If he moves right off without any leg aids, let him go without using your legs, until he comes to a complete stop. If he heads for home, steer him away from the barn before he gets very close to it. Resist the urge to give him any leg or crop signals, even if he slows to a crawl. All you are asking, for now, is that he move at all.

When the horse stops, or if he hasn't budged since you got on, give him an ordinary leg signal (a squeeze, not a kick), with one leg. Keep squeezing with that leg, until the horse moves—in any direction. Reward the horse by releasing the leg pressure for any movement of his feet, even if it's only one step with one foot. You can also use voice commands with your leg signal if that helps, but the horse should learn to obey the leg signal by itself as well.

If the horse still hasn't moved and your leg feels like it's going to fall off, switch the pressure to the other leg, with no break for the horse. When both legs are tired, use the end of your crop or a stick behind your leg in a poking pressure.

If the horse backs up instead of moving forward, or tries to do a turn on the forehand, reward him anyway, and then repeat the pressure. Sooner or later he will get tired of going around in circles or backwards, and he will go forward.

When the horse takes one step forward, your battle (although not the war) has been won. He has moved forward because of your leg pressure. Reward him for that first step immediately (as soon as he begins the step) by releasing the pressure. Now you must be very careful to convince him that moving when you ask him is a comfortable thing to do. Keep your reins loose at this time, and don't give him any leg signals as long as he is moving, even if it is very slow. (You can use your body signals.) If the horse starts off fast, don't pull him down until you have to, and then do so gently and reward him quickly for slowing down. He *must* get a reward for obeying or you haven't taught him anything.

Depending on your horse, you may want to keep working the horse until he will move fairly soon after you apply the leg pressure. If he has been very stubborn about it you may want to quit the lesson as soon as he takes one or two steps. Tomorrow you can expect a little more, but for now, be satisfied with any progress at all.

The next day repeat the procedure carefully and do it each time you ride until the horse has learned that you will stop squeezing as soon as he moves. Don't kick the horse because the end of each kick is a reward and you can't time them with his movements.

With time and absolute patience, any horse should eventually become fairly responsive. Of course, if the horse has been allowed to get away with being sluggish and slow for years, and if he is fairly insensitive to pain or pressure anyway, you might be better off selling him. You should be able to tell within a week or two if this is the case.

If your horse does not respond to this treatment, make sure you have been doing it right before you give up on him. Change your ways of signaling, try him in different places, or try a different bit. If you have been using anything but a plain snaffle on him, change to a snaffle or bosal on the chance that he is afraid of the bit. If you can't get your legs against the horse well in your saddle (some Western saddles are made so you cannot use your legs properly), either change to an English saddle for a while, ride bareback for a while, or take your feet out of the stirrups and bring your legs farther back than usual. Be inventive, try new things. If what you are doing makes your horse mad (he flattens his ears, switches his tail, or tries to buck), try something else. Hurting him or making him mad will not teach him that being ridden is good for him: it will only make him worse.

While some horses don't like to move with a rider, there

are those that won't stop once they get going. Some of them have both problems, and are practically hopeless, or so it seems.

The kind of horse that runs away usually follows a pattern just as the balker does. Horses run away for two reasons: either they have gotten into the habit because they know they can get away with it, or they are frightened into running away by a bad rider. The horse that bolts occasionally because of a frightening obstacle on the trail, or some unusual occurrence, does not fall into this category. The type of horse that runs away on purpose is usually more of a bother than he is dangerous. Once you get him out of a walk, or perhaps just when he's in a canter, his head goes down, and off he goes, paying no attention to your pulling on his mouth. He'll run back to the barn, over to the gate, or up to the horse ahead of him. Sometimes this kind of horse doesn't even bother to actually run—he just canters home. He is seemingly unresponsive to any kind of bit. You can't stop him, and he knows it. He has you "buffaloed."

The nervous, frightened runaway is more of a problem in a way, since he may be dangerous. He is high-headed and nervous by nature. He often has Thoroughbred, Arab, or Saddlebred characteristics, although this is not always the case. One nearly always sees severe bits on this kind of horse, and these bits can actually contribute to the horse's problem. An inexperienced rider on a spirited horse may resort to a heavier bit because the horse has more energy than the rider can handle. Most people think that if a horse is hard to stop, the solution is to put a stronger bit on him, because he has a "hard" mouth and can't feel a regular bit. However, it is important to realize that if a bit is misused the horse doesn't respond to it because he can't understand the signals. If a rider doesn't give signals properly, leans forward when he wants to slow down, keeps pulling even after the horse has slowed down or stopped, or pulls the reins most of the time or at odd moments when no signal is meant, the horse gets so confused that a pull on the mouth no longer tells him to stop. If stopping doesn't relieve the pressure and pain in his mouth, he may try to outrun it. This, of course, causes more pulling by the rider, but the poor horse can't reason well enough to figure this out. The more the rider pulls, the faster the horse must run. If he makes it back to the barn or otherwise gets the rider off, he learns that the solution to a pain in the mouth is to run fast to get rid of the rider. The more severe the bit becomes, the more nervous and upset the horse gets, and the worse his manners become.

Each of these two types of runaways must be treated differently. Handling the nervous type with the wrong treatment could be disastrous, so it is important to determine which type your runaway is and how steady his nerves are before you try to correct the problem.

For the purposeful type of runaway, a little ingenuity is required. Find an enclosed area to ride the horse in if possible. If he never runs away in a ring or enclosure, you'll have to do this where he does run away. When the horse starts to take off with you, if you are in a ring, you can do one of several things. You could make him keep going, round and round the ring, until he is thoroughly tired of running and wants to stop. Or you can turn him in as small a circle as you can make and keep making the circle smaller and smaller until he has to come back down to a walk. If you are out of the ring and he takes off, turn him around so he is heading away from the barn, if you can. If you can't turn him around, let him go until he gets to the barn and either turn him around and make him go back, or ride him back and forth in front of the barn for a while. If you can keep him from stopping completely, you may be able to trot him away from the barn again. The idea is to keep him going and not let him rest at the barn. If you have to, get off and lead him away, but get back on and keep on riding. Even if you have to spend all of a few rides riding back and forth or around the barn, eventually the horse will realize that he is not getting out of work by running to the barn.

If the rider of this kind of horse is a small child, you may have to get someone bigger and stronger to correct this habit, and then have the bigger person periodically ride the horse to keep him from reverting. If the horse persists in taking advantage of the small child's inability to control him, you may have to find another, more suitable horse.

The nervous, high-headed horse presents a different problem, but in some cases may be easier to cure than the purposeful runaway. The first thing to remember is that someone, perhaps you, got the horse into this state. This means that he has been mishandled and must be ridden sensibly and carefully in order to overcome his fears about being ridden. If you have just gotten this horse and he was like that when you got him, you can assume that someone else has gotten him into this shape. However, if you have had him a while, or if he has gotten worse since you have had him, then you must be at least partly at fault. Even considering that the horse may have had a nervous temperament to start with, your riding habits have made him this way.

You should sit down and evaluate the way you ride and make plans to alter your habits. Do you have a tendency to run all the time, seldom taking the time to just walk for a while and enjoy the scenery or the weather? Do you "hot rod" your horse, making fast starts and sliding stops all the time? Do you *ever* race with your friends? How quiet and relaxed are you in the stable and in handling the horse from the ground? Do you secretly think it's neat to have a hot-headed excitable horse in order to impress people with your riding ability? Whatever you have been doing, it is time to reevaluate and start over.

First, slow down and establish a calm, relaxed relationship with your horse. Spend a little more time grooming him and just talking to him and leading him around. Take your time in handling him and tack him up slowly and carefully instead of just throwing the saddle on and hopping on.

Look over your tack carefully. Make sure the saddle fits and is padded adequately. Check the horse's girth area after each ride for lumps or hot spots that mean the girth is pinching. Get rid of whatever harsh bit you are using. Find or buy a snaffle or other mild bit. If you are using a mild curb, try using a snaffle for a while to change the position of the bit in the horse's mouth. Change to a curb strap instead of chain, if you use one, at least temporarily. If you are using a tie-down or martingale, either take it off or loosen it up a few notches, as you probably have it pulled too tight. Unless the horse is a confirmed rearer, you should probably take it off entirely.

This kind of horse may work better out of a ring, particularly if you have been barrel racing him or otherwise exciting him in a confined place. However, if it does not excite him, you may feel safer in a ring.

From the time you go out to ride your horse, you should have in mind a quiet, slow ride. This kind of horse needs slow, relaxing work for a period of time, possibly even for a year or so. I bought a young mare once that had been ruined by being raced all the time. Although she was quiet and easy to handle on the ground, she turned into a wild thing when I got on and picked up the reins. It took a full year of retraining before anyone could ride her without her "blowing up." So be prepared to be patient and to take some time solving this problem.

You should also realize that if the horse has a nervous disposition to start with and has been handled poorly for years, he may never settle down enough for you, or at least not until he's twenty-five years old! If he is a child's horse, unless he is very quiet and reasonable to handle on the ground, it is unlikely that he will calm down enough to be suitable for the young rider.

Start all rides by tacking up slowly and leading the horse around for a few minutes before mounting. Each time you go to ride, pretend that the horse has never been ridden before and that you must be very careful not to excite him. If the horse is so nervous about being ridden that he reacts nervously to being saddled, spend a week or two just tacking and untacking him, without getting on at all, until the sight of a saddle no longer frightens him.

Once you have tacked up and walked around, stop the horse and just stand there for a few minutes. Wait until he has relaxed and is no longer anxiously awaiting your getting on before you mount.

When you do mount, do so in a place where the horse cannot move off (in front of a fence or even in the stall, if necessary) and just sit there on him for a few minutes instead of moving off. If the horse is very nervous and raises his head or fidgets when you are just sitting on him, spend a few days just standing around and not riding at all. Get on in different places, if possible, and just sit there for ten or fifteen minutes, or until the horse relaxes. Do this until the horse no longer stiffens up and raises his head when you get on.

Once the horse accepts being mounted without getting

excited, it is time to start riding *at a walk*. Start the horse off with a slightly loose rein and a very relaxed seat. Force yourself to relax even if you're scared to death, or have someone else ride the horse for a while to get you over this. However, you will have to learn to relax if you ever want to ride this particular horse and have him be relaxed. Use as light aids as possible and voice commands only, if you can. Pretend your reins are made of thread; hold them very lightly. Keep your hands low, so your fingers just brush the mane in front of the withers. If you ride Western keep your hand down in front of the saddle horn. Don't let your hands come up higher than a few inches over the neck. Most excitable horses have a problem with keeping their heads too high anyway.

Walk the horse slowly and calmly, talking to him. Let him walk at his own speed as long as he will move calmly. If he starts to jog or prance, stop him *gently,* talking to him quietly, or circle him slowly until he slows down again, if he will do it calmly. Do *not* lean forward. When the horse does stop, let him stand, talk to him, and stroke his neck. When he has settled down completely (and he will quickly if your work at standing was thorough enough) either try walking again, if he seems calm enough, or quit for the day. Stay calm and talk to him in quiet, soothing tones. If you feel you are losing your temper or otherwise getting excited, get off and quit for the day. If the horse "blows up" (gets very excited, or rears) get off and lead him around for a few minutes and try again, or quit for the day, whichever you think is better.

If you haven't been riding the horse very much and he doesn't stay out at pasture during the day, you may need to longe him for an hour or so each day to work the excess energy out of him. Longeing him for half an hour or so before each ride may help keep him calm when you ride him, although if you continue this for a long period of time he may come to expect it and will be unruly when he isn't longed.

Take the horse out and ride him at a walk for only as long as it takes him to learn to remain relaxed the whole time you are on him. Stop and stand him often and dismount and get back on several times during each ride. Ride for a half hour or longer at each ride, if the horse will tolerate it.

While all this walking may bore you at first, after a while you should begin to relax and enjoy it, and you should begin to get to know and like your horse better. If your horse doesn't get plenty of exercise in the pasture, you should longe him every day at faster gaits than a walk to keep him fit during this period of slow riding. When you ride, look for hills to walk up and down and other rough (but safe) terrain to help keep up his muscle tone.

When you are *sure* that your horse is ready, take him to an arena or other place where there are no distractions for your trotting. Don't rush him into it, as trotting before he has thoroughly calmed down at a walk may set him back to where you started. When you're ready to trot, shorten your reins so you can make contact with the horse's mouth without raising your hands. If your horse responds to voice commands (and he should if you longe him) give him a voice command only to trot, for a while at least. It might be wise to sit the trot, rather than post, to encourage the horse to keep it slow. If the horse starts off too fast, don't jerk back on him; pull gently or turn him in a small circle.

For the first few days at least, trot the horse only once or twice during each ride. Keep your trotting down to only a few times per ride for at least a week or two. You should be walking twice as much as you trot anyway, at least for most pleasure riding

As long as your horse remains calm you can gradually increase the length and frequency of your trotting. If the horse gets excited, however, go back to walking or trotting only for short periods of time until he settles down again. The length of time it takes to get the horse trotting calmly will depend on his temperament and on your careful treatment. The duration of the horse's previous mistreatment will have some bearing on it too, and you can expect this retraining to take longer if the horse has been like this for several years. If the horse is over six or seven years of age it may also take longer, and a horse over ten years or so may never be able to change his habits enough to become really calm and settled down. If you have an older horse that is really hot-headed and you want to sell him and get a calmer horse, you may want to use this treatment for a while before you sell him. This way he will be easier to sell because his manners will have improved, and you can feel better knowing that he is at least somewhat better behaved. Don't sell this horse to a beginner, though!

You should not even consider cantering your excitable horse until he walks and trots completely calmly, without raising his head or getting "hot." As I said, this may take as long as a year. But if the horse is progressing and is really becoming calm and sensible, it will be worth the wait, for with careful riding his whole personality and way of going will improve and he will become even better and more dependable as time goes on.

If you have been working with the horse for several months and he is not improving noticeably, you should stop and examine your methods. Is the horse getting enough exercise to keep him from being nervous just from excess energy? Is someone else riding him who is undoing your work? (This program cannot work unless everyone who rides the horse follows it carefully all of the time.) Have there been times when you said to yourself, "Oh, one day can't hurt," and went ahead and rode in your usual way instead of trying to keep it down to just a walk and trot, or even just went about the whole thing in a nervous or grouchy mood? Sometimes this can ruin weeks of work just by worrying the horse. The horse has a much longer memory than you do. Generally, he will remember bad things (a jerk on the mouth, an angry kick) much longer than the good things you are trying to teach him. He may be still worrying about the bit and tossing his head around. If you haven't changed bits, it may bother him just to have it in his mouth. A different bit may relax him and stop him from remembering the pain of the old one.

Only when the horse walks and trots calmly, and stops and turns well, is it time to think about cantering. As before, be calm and slow about it. You should probably start the horse out at a slow trot and then ease him into a canter, rather than trying a canter depart from a walk. Give the horse as light a signal as you can, and only let him canter for a few strides before easing him back to a trot and then to a walk. Canter only once in a while for a time, then gradually work up to a normal amount. Be careful to keep your starts and stops gradual and relaxed. Don't make the mistake of "letting him run it out," since allowing him to run will only make him worse.

Once the horse is working at all gaits calmly again, your job is not over. Retraining an excitable horse is like going on a diet: once you have reached your goal you must work to stay there, or you'll only end up right back where you started. You must keep your habits changed to sensible ones so the horse doesn't go back to being jumpy and hot-headed.

Put yourself on a program, if necessary, to keep things going smoothly. Make it an invariable habit to walk the first five minutes and the last five minutes of every ride.

Tack up and mount at a leisurely pace; no hurry-up jobs just to get going. Make it a point to walk at least as much as you canter. Don't "cowboy" your starts and stops: make them gradual. Take the time to stop and stand several times on each ride, go out of your way to walk on completely loose reins in a relaxed manner, mount and dismount often. Keep any routine riding varied so the horse doesn't learn to anticipate movements and become excited.

Much of the problem with an excitable horse comes from riding with friends who want to race, or just riding with other horses in a manner that excites your horse. When you ride with friends, take turns being the leader and the last horse in line. This will insure that the horse won't get so he will fret and fuss if he isn't in front, and that he will learn to follow a group. Also put him in the middle of the group part of the time, unless he is a confirmed kicker. Even so, if you ride sensibly and keep a proper distance between horses, a kicker needn't get an opportunity to endanger anyone.

Never race your horse with another at a gallop. Occasionally walking or trotting races can be fun, but it is asking for trouble to race at full speed. Avoid riding abreast when heading for home or within sight of home as it encourages the horses to want to race. At other times, riding abreast part of the time can be beneficial to the horse's training as it teaches him to pace himself with another horse and not to fret when another horse comes alongside. However, too much of this may hurt you if you plan to show, as your horse may learn to hang alongside other horses instead of passing them in the ring.

When you ride in company, always warn those behind you when you start into a faster gait. This will keep their horses from trying to bolt after you. Ask them to do the same for you. Also warn them before you slow down, and work out an emergency stopping signal before you begin a ride, in case you come across an obstacle suddenly.

If you are following someone, don't let your horse just start off behind him on his own without a signal. If he tries to bolt forward, turn him around so he is facing in the opposite direction. Double him if necessary. If you want to catch up to someone, do so at a trot, not a run. Pull up well in advance of when you have to stop and trot up slowly to a group or another horse.

Sometimes riding with another horse can help an excitable horse calm down. If you have a friend with a slow, quiet horse, riding alongside him at a walk and trot may help your horse learn to go slowly and calmly. If riding in company makes your horse worse, however, you are better off riding alone until he is calm before you test him with a friend.

I think I hear more complaints about leads than about anything else in riding. Most of the trouble seems to stem from the horse being naturally right or left "handed." When the horse is running and playing loose, you may notice him using one lead most or all of the time. Sometimes this is a lifelong habit, but it may also be the result of an injury or weakness in one hind leg that makes the horse favor it and use the other one more often. If the rider is not observant enough to catch the beginning of one-sidedness, it may become a real problem.

From the time you first get a horse you should notice which lead he tends to favor. If you are lucky enough to get a horse that doesn't have a favorite side, you should carefully preserve this desirable state.

One thing that contributes to a horse developing the habit of favoring one side is riding lopsided in the saddle. This causes the horse to work more on the side the rider is leaning to, thus developing those muscles more fully.

Since the rider's balance is off to one side, it may take a conscious effort on the part of the rider to overcome this tendency until the habit is broken.

One way to avoid leaning is to make sure you straighten the saddle and sit in the middle of the horse's back each time you ride. Check to make sure that the pommel of the saddle lines up with the horse's mane, that the center of the saddle follows the center line of the horse's back, and that your seat corresponds with both the middle of the saddle and the horse's spine. Then you need to check periodically during your rides to make sure you have not gotten out of alignment. Check the length of your stirrups to make sure they're exactly even as that can throw you off balance without your even realizing it. With English stirrups it may be difficult to tell if they are just one notch off, but you can always measure them with a tape.

The other thing that makes a horse one-sided is working more in one direction than the other and turning one way more than the other. Many riders unconsciously turn to the left most of the time, for instance, because they hold the reins in the left hand and it is easier to neckrein to that direction. Sometimes a rider does this without realizing it because the horse is easier to turn to his favorite side.

If your horse is already one-sided when you get him, or if you now realize that he is like this, you will need to start working him more in the direction that is his "bad" side until he is developed equally. It should not take long to correct this tendency in a young horse, but if the horse is aged (over 10 years) and has been this way for years, you may never be able to completely overcome it. You may always have trouble getting on one lead as the difference in muscular development is permanent.

If you have problems with leads with your horse and he is not definitely one-sided, the problem may be yours. The horse is probably at fault if he never takes one of his leads, or almost never, but if he just misses leads on either side some of the time, or if it takes two or three tries to get one lead, the problem is probably that you are not giving the signals at the right time or have the horse positioned wrong to take the lead you ask for.

The horse must be aligned properly in order to be able to take the lead you want. His body must be either perfectly straight or at such an angle that he can push off with his outside hind foot. If the horse is turned so that the wrong hind foot is ahead, however slight the inclination, he will be unable to take the lead you ask for. When the rider signals for a canter while the horse is misaligned, the horse must either take a few strides and correct himself before he can pick up the right lead, or he will go right into the wrong lead. The rider should not give the cantering signal until the horse's hind legs are following the tracks of the front feet exactly, or the hind quarters are slightly toward the center of the ring or the side of the lead you want. You can align the horse by using your outside leg to move the hindquarters over slightly and by using light rein pressure to pull the horse's head *slightly* to the side away from the lead wanted, if this is needed to help bring his hindquarters in. However, you should be careful not to pull his head out too far.

When a horse has gotten into the habit of taking only one lead, he will resist the efforts of the rider to align him correctly. Or he will shift his position quickly between the time the signal is given and the actual canter depart. He usually does this by taking two or three trotting steps before getting into the canter.

The rider with a lead problem should probably work in a ring or other arena for a while until the problem is solved, or use a straight stretch of fence in the pasture. Sometimes it is virtually impossible to get the horse aligned

To take the proper lead, the horse must be aligned so that he can push off with the outside hind leg (opposite to the lead desired). The horse's hindquarters should be just a little closer to the inside of the circle than his shoulder. In this picture the horse is pushing off with the outside hind leg in preparation for a canter on the right lead.

properly without the visual and physical aid of a fence. Even if you don't have a ring, you will need to work the horse in a circle to get him to take the lead he doesn't like.

To get a horse to take his "bad" lead, you will probably have to exaggerate both the alignment of his body and the signal used to ask for a canter. You will have to force him into the position from which he must take the lead you want. Sometimes this can be done by starting the horse into a canter right on a turn, keeping him as close to the fence as you can safely get, and keeping his head as close to the fence as possible. This should prevent him from pushing off with the inside hind leg, which would put him on the wrong lead.

If your horse is agile enough to do flying changes of lead (without breaking into a trot) you may be able to force him to get on the bad lead by turning him in a very small circle at a canter, in the direction of the lead you want to take. If the circle becomes small enough, he will have to change leads to keep his balance. This method has several disadvantages, however, that may crop up with certain types of horses. One is that the horse may become "disunited," which means cantering on one lead in the front and the other in the back. You can feel this because the horse's canter becomes very rough and shaky. You may be able to correct this by pulling the horse up, just to a trot, and then kicking him back up into a canter after only one trotting stride, which should put him on the right lead. The other disadvantage is that unless the horse is very responsive, he may just break to a trot and refuse to canter when the circle gets very small.

Once you have gotten the horse on the right lead, even if by accident, praise him, work him a couple of times around the ring or circle, then stop, cool him out, and put him away. Do this for several days or until he begins to take the bad lead more often. Gradually increase the amount of cantering done on the bad lead until you are working that side about twice as much as the other. Do this until he will take either lead equally well. Don't neglect the good side entirely, however, or the horse may switch sides and become stiff on that one instead. Some people recommend that once you get the horse on his bad lead you should keep him on it for a long time, to build it up, but I find that if you work on it too much at one time in the beginning, it tires the horse out and makes him sore. He's then even less likely to want to go on that lead. How much work the bad lead needs will depend on how old the horse is and how much of a habit the one-sidedness has become.

If the horse is very persistent about taking the wrong lead and so agile that he can canter in a very small circle without changing, there is another method that might work. Ride the horse down the fence on the straightaway in the direction of his good lead. Keep him far enough away from the fence so you can turn him around toward the fence. Walk him almost down to the curve in the ring, then whirl him and give him a very strong cantering signal just *before* he completes the full turn to the opposite direction. This is to force him to jump into the canter on the correct lead by pushing off with the outside hind leg. This may not work on a horse that doesn't respond quickly to leg or crop signals.

You may have to use a bit of ingenuity to get a one-sided horse to take his bad lead. You should keep in mind, too, that unless you are going to show your horse, it might not really matter if he doesn't take one lead, if you enjoy him and he can do the things you want him to.

Another common complaint is about the horse that won't back. Again, the difficulty usually comes from the rider mishandling the horse. While backing is not a natural movement to the horse (when loose he seldom, if ever, gets himself in a position where he must back up) it can be taught relatively easily. Most riders find that if they get into a spot where it is really necessary to back up, their horse will do it almost on his own. Then they discover that he won't do it when they are just practicing. This is because the horse was backing the first time by instinct, not because he was trained to do it.

Most problems with backing arise because the rider gives conflicting or confusing signals and doesn't reward the horse for moving backwards. Many horses develop rearing problems from being yanked back on a severe bit while being kicked in the ribs; others learn to resist by opening the mouth, raising the head, or turning the head to one side.

If you have a horse that won't back, it probably doesn't matter too much whether he has been spoiled or just not trained to back. He should be retrained anyway. You can teach him to back no matter which way he resists, even if he rears.

If the horse tries to rear when you back him, you are probably using too much bit and too much leg. Change him to a snaffle or to as mild a bit as you can find. If you cannot buy or borrow a mild bit or absolutely cannot control him at all on less bit than you are now using, you will have to develop the ability to use the bit you have very, very gently. Do not try to use any leg pressure when trying to back a horse that rears.

Before you can teach the horse to back you must learn the procedure thoroughly. Teaching the horse to back must be done slowly, carefully, and with patience. If it is done correctly, the horse will learn it in a short time and as long as the signals are given correctly he will back smoothly and without raising his head, because if your signals are correct he won't mind backing.

You must teach your horse to stand quietly before you can expect him to back properly. Practice stopping and standing for a few minutes in various places until the horse doesn't fret or sidestep when he is supposed to be standing.

When you begin to teach the horse to back, do not expect him to back several strides at a time. A step or two at first is plenty. Once he has the idea, you can increase the backing each time until he strides back smoothly.

Before you try to back the horse you should learn what the horse does when he backs. The most important thing to know is that the horse must arch his back in order to back, just as he does over a jump. He must have his head in the right position in order to be able to do this. A horse *cannot* back if his head is in such a position that he cannot arch his back (such as high in the air with the nose pointing up). The ideal position for arching the back is with the head flexed at the poll and the face nearly perpendicular to the ground. With the head in this position the horse will find it easy to step back with diagonal legs.

If your horse does not flex at the poll when you take up on the reins, you must teach him to do this. It really

When the horse backs, he tucks his head and arches his back. The rider should stand slightly in the stirrups to facilitate the movement of the horse's back. The hands should be kept low and the legs, if used, should guide the hindquarters, not push the horse forward.

isn't hard to do, and you can begin the training on the ground. Stand beside the horse's head, facing forward, and hold one rein in each hand several inches behind and a few inches above the bit. Using equal pressure on each rein, pull gently with a steady pressure. This is one time when you don't want give-and-take pressure. Watch the horse's head, especially his jaw, carefully. Watch for him to tuck his chin to get away from the pressure of the bit. As soon as he tucks *at all,* even one inch, instantly release the pressure to reward him. If he raises his head or does anything else except tuck, keep pulling with the same amount of pressure. Be careful not to release the pressure when the horse has his head up or to one side, as this rewards him for having his head out of position. Normally a horse will learn this very quickly, and you should have him tucking well after his first fifteen minute lesson.

When the horse is tucking well in hand, you can try it mounted. The first few lessons may need to be devoted only to tucking, without attempting to back at all. Don't try to back the horse before he is tucking, as you will teach him to back with his head out of position and sooner or later he will begin to resist because this isn't comfortable. If the horse backs readily without tucking, and keeps his head out of position, you may want to "set his head." This means tying the reins to the saddle or girth at a length that causes him to tuck slightly to relieve the pressure on his mouth. Leave him in the head set for half an hour or so a day until he doesn't fight it at all any more. (Make sure the reins are of an even length.) This may teach the horse not to move his head out of position. If it doesn't, try using less rein pressure on the mouth, with slight leg pressure to keep him from backing.

Once the horse has learned to tuck when you are mounted, you can begin backing. You may be able to do

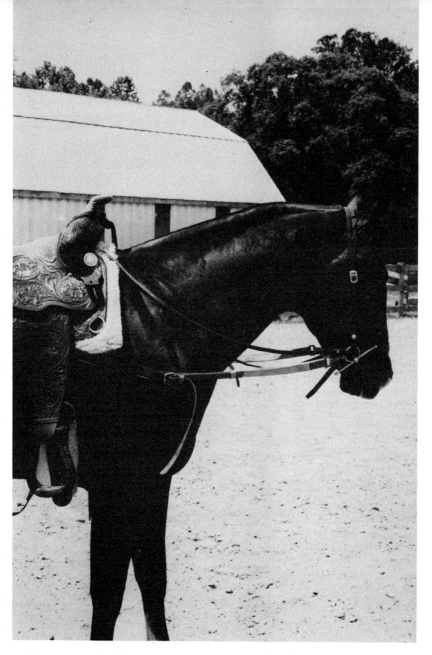

Flexing at the poll, the horse in side reins (bitting rig). The horse can be taught to flex at the poll at rein pressure by tying side reins to the saddle as shown. You can then turn the horse loose to figure out for himself that if he pulls on the reins they pull back.

this the same day you began tucking while mounted if your horse is cooperative and your touch is right. To ask the horse to back, first tuck him and reward by slackening the pressure just enough to reward but not enough to lose the tuck. Rest for a count of five to reward him, and then ask for a step back by pulling gently on *one* rein. This can be accompanied by light pressure with the opposite leg, since the horse steps backward with diagonal legs. When the horse takes one step backward, reward him by releasing the pressure. At first release completely and start over; later you can release very slightly, count to five, then ask with the other rein and leg for another step. Soon the

The horse fights the reins, but they don't release. The advantage of a bitting rig is that it never makes a mistake—it never releases at the wrong time, and never pulls at the wrong time.

After a while, the horse learns to accept the bit, holding the head in such a position that it does not pull. This teaches the horse to tuck his head at rein pressure.

horse should progress to taking smooth strides backward to your alternating hand and leg signals.

Some horses may find it easier to back if you shift your weight slightly forward so they can arch their backs more easily. This is particularly true with a large rider on a small horse. Do not lean forward, however, as the horse will take this as a signal to move forward. If you have trouble with the horse trying to walk forward, stand him facing a fence for the first few lessons until he gets the message.

Use the voice command "Back" liberally when training

and backing and your horse may learn to back for it alone.

If the horse does not tuck when you ask him to, keep up a steady pull with both reins until he does, no matter what else he does with his head. If the horse starts to rear, double him quickly *before* you release the pressure, or you will have taught him that rearing gets the reward of release. Your pull was probably too hard in the first place, or he wouldn't have reared. Calm him down and try a lighter pull. If your horse is so spoiled that he rears every time you pull at all, you may be able to break him of this. Rather than trying to tie his head down, try "draw reins." You can use two lead shanks six to eight feet long or two pieces of soft rope. Fasten one end of each rope to the cinch ring or girth at a level with the horse's mouth when his head is at a normal, resting level. Run each draw rein through the bit ring and to the saddle. This way when you pull on the horse's mouth, it pulls his head down towards the cinch ring with leverage. CAUTION: USE DRAW REINS ONLY WITH A PLAIN JOINTED SNAFFLE BIT AS THEY CAN HURT HIS MOUTH IF HE RESISTS.

Ride the horse around for a while with the draw reins so he gets a little used to them before you try backing him with them. Then stand him in front of a fence, sit forward, and try to back him, using only as much pull as necessary. Be patient and be quick to reward the horse for good head position. With a horse that throws his head up when the reins are pulled, reward him when he puts it back down, even if it isn't tucked, until he stops throwing it up.

Use draw reins only as a last resort; they can be very severe. You can also use them on a horse that doesn't turn well, as they give the rider leverage.

Be careful not to reward the horse for opening his mouth. Sometimes you can't tell whether he's opened his mouth or tucked his chin, and if you reward him for opening his mouth, it may become a firm habit which is very hard to break. Have someone watch him for you, and reward only for tucking with the mouth closed. If you accept opening the mouth for tucking, he may never get out of it.

Many people claim that some horses are built so they can't flex at the poll and tuck the chin. However, *any* horse can do it, and if yours seems to have trouble with it, a head set may be necessary.

If your horse seems to be confused by your leg signals and wants to move forward or insists on turning his hindquarters away from your leg, you may be better off not using any leg pressure at all when backing. Some horses back much better with no leg aids, and others will back with legs only. You should experiment a little and find out how your horse feels about it. If the horse gets excited and moves his head out of position, you will have to start all over again.

Once you have taught the horse to back correctly you should have no more problems until you get sloppy and start backing him wrong. Getting impatient and hauling back on the reins may get him to back the first few times, but sooner or later he will begin to resist, and you will have lost control of his backing. You will then have to start all over again.

Leaving the barn or stable area is another problem, particularly for young riders on big horses, and for inexperienced riders. It's asking a lot to expect a horse to leave his stablemates and grass or hay by himself. In a group things usually go smoothly, but more often than not there is no one for the horse to follow out that gate or up road. Most horses exhibit at least some reluctance to go out, even well trained ones. It may come in the form of an ear cocked back, a slightly slower gait, or the horse may simply plant his feet and refuse to move. He may zigzag, throw his head around, try to rear, or whirl around to head for home.

Different things work with different horses, but there are generally a few things you can find to do about this problem. Walking the horse around in front of the barn and then starting out at a trot may give him enough momentum to keep going until he is out of the problem area. Using a crop smartly on his side a few times and using loud, firm (downright nasty, sometimes) voice commands and strong legs may intimidate him into giving up the battle and moving out. I find the voice command "Git!" useful at this time. If the horse won't go forward but keeps whirling around, spinning him in circles in both directions until you are both dizzy and then using your legs and voice strongly may do it. A horse that really rears is a dangerous problem, and the best thing to do may be to get off and lead him for a while or have someone lead him out with you on him.

A rider can usually learn to anticipate when the horse is going to rear and may be able to prevent him from doing it by spinning him. The horse will tense the muscles in his back and hindquarters when he is about to rear and also may crouch a little. Sometimes a sharp crack on the rump will make him jump forward instead of to the rear, if he is caught at the right moment. However, no one but an experienced rider should attempt to cope with a rearing horse. A horse that cannot be broken of this habit should be sold.

Then there is the horse that bucks, or at least kicks up his heels, when you hit him with the crop. If you are good enough to stay on, you may be able to whip him out of this, but usually it is better to change tactics and stop using your crop.

Patience is the great key to the horse that balks. IF you can stand it, sooner or later you can wait him out and get him to move. Do it on a day when you have plenty of time and just sit there until he gets tired of the inactivity. (Keep him awake, though, or he'll just have a nice nap!) When he does move, praise him and pet him so he knows he did something right. Nothing will make a horse rebel faster than having someone kick and pound on him no matter what he does, so reward him for good behavior.

Once you have gotten the horse past the problem area, make sure you regain at least some of the composure you lost in making him go. Be nice to him and make his ride as pleasant as possible, or he will resist even harder the next time you try to ride.

CHAPTER 9

Common Problems
with Form

Many people ride for years and never worry about how they look on their horses. Others, who want to show, worry about it from the first day they ride. What is form, anyway? It is the position of the rider on the horse, the way you sit, hold your arms and hands, the position of your legs and feet. In addition, it is how well you hold this position through the various movements the horse performs. Good form is necessary to good riding, for noticeable deviations from the established rules of form put the rider out of balance and interfere with his control of the horse. However, there is room within the guidelines of form for individual variation.

If you have a problem with your form, or someone mentions to you that you don't look right, it will probably worry you, but trying to correct a fault without help may make things worse. First, try to have someone take a picture of you riding (movies if possible) or try to find a place with a large mirror set up in an arena so you can see yourself ride. This is invaluable, as you can see both the problem and how modifying your position affects it.

You may want to find someone to give you lessons for a while, to correct problems or just "polish up" your form. However, this can either be a blessing or it can make things worse. Your instructor must be someone who is knowledgeable about horses and riding, can get his/her ideas across clearly, and who generally agrees with your concept of riding. This last point is less important with a beginning rider or young child perhaps, but a more experienced rider or adult may find himself in conflict with the ideas of his instructor, and this may negate the good done by having an observer. It is also especially important to pick an instructor whom the child likes for a child.

One of the most common problems with form is that of balance. This problem is common with riders who have not had professional instruction, as they may learn to ride in an incorrect position without realizing it. Sometimes developing a secure grip with the legs or an ability to balance on the horse by the "seat of the pants" enables the rider to stay on easily without being balanced *with* the horse. Sometimes seeing yourself in a photograph may jolt you into realizing that you are either leaning way over the horse's neck (ahead of the horse) or sitting too far back with your feet shoved forward (behind the horse). Many times a rider is unable to feel this problem until he is taught to sit properly. Then he says, "How did I ever ride like that without falling off?" Of course, if you practiced long enough you could learn to ride on one knee sitting backwards, but that doesn't make it the correct way to ride.

Balance problems often come from having the stirrups too short. People who are taught to ride forward seat or who try to learn it from books often hike their stirrups up very short on the theory that they have to have them that short in order to balance over the withers properly. While it is true that you need your stirrups one or two notches shorter than I recommend in order to ride forward seat properly, some people have them four to six notches too short. Having the stirrups too short does one of two things to the rider: either he must lean too far forward perched over his toes to keep his legs under him, or he slides back and lets his feet move up "on the dashboard."

To tell whether your stirrups are the right length, sit with your seat midway between the pommel and cantle of the saddle, and hang your legs straight down as if you were trying to touch the ground. Your stirrups should reach so the bottoms of them are just even with the bottom of your foot or your ankle bone, whichever you prefer. You can check this by having someone hold the stirrup against your leg or you can gently swing your legs back and forth against the horse's sides so the stirrups hit your legs. Don't reach down and hold the stirrup against your leg as this changes its relation to your foot. You will probably discover that your stirrups were several inches too short. I've known people who rode for years with their stirrups six to eight inches too short. They're amazed at how much more comfortable and easy riding becomes when their legs aren't cramped up under them.

If your stirrups measure correctly but you still have trouble being out of balance, try lowering them a notch or two anyway. People with very short legs sometimes find it easier to ride with longer stirrups, while a long-legged slender person may often be comfortable with stirrups that measure shorter on their legs.

After you have adjusted your stirrups, if you have been having a problem with being too far forward, try making an effort to sit up straight and to sit down in the saddle and relax. Leaning over the pommel or horn, in addition to throwing your weight too far forward, often makes a rider tense. It also makes the horse think you are giving him a constant signal to speed up. Your body should be nearly perpendicular to the ground at all gaits except at the gallop and when jumping, when you should lean slightly forward.

If you have been riding behind your horse, lowering your stirrups should help you sit more forward in your saddle. Sometimes it helps to practice riding without stirrups or bareback. Another method that might help is to ride for short periods with your eyes closed. Try this in a ring or other place where the horse will go without guidance, and you will be surprised at how different it feels! If you feel very off balance, then you probably need to work without stirrups or bareback to develop your balance. You cannot depend on grip and holding on to keep you on the horse, and good balance makes riding much easier both for you and the horse.

Another common problem riders have is bouncing. Some bounce just at a canter, some bounce all the time. Some riders can keep their seats on the saddle but their legs start swinging back and forth. Then if they tighten up their legs their bottom bounces up and down or back and forth. They despair at ever having the kind of seat that stays "glued to the saddle." You'd be surprised at how simple the solution is. I was plagued for years with this problem, and I thought that I would never become a "good" enough rider to stop bouncing. However, the secret is not in being good enough, but in being *relaxed* enough. Bouncing, jerking, and swinging legs are all caused by the rider being too tense and stiff in the lower back and hips, and sometimes even in the knees. Being able to sit a horse's gaits without moving off the saddle or having parts of the body swinging around comes with relaxing the body so it moves *with* the horse instead of against him.

As you ride at a walk, concentrate on relaxing your whole body. At first let yourself overdo it, becoming as limp as possible without actually sliding to the ground in a heap. Be the original "sack of meal" for a while. Then gradually tighten your shoulders and back just enough to attain good posture. Keep your arms relaxed so they can swing back and forth with the motion of the horse's head. Tighten your ankles so your heels are down, but keep your knees relaxed so that they can absorb the jar of the horse's gaits. Much of the bouncing and too-high posting you see in riders is caused by stiff knees and ankles. Your hips should be relaxed and moving forward and back with the motion of the horse. The only time the hips and waist should be tightened up is when you are asking the horse to slow down or stop. Remember that when you are not moving with the horse you are moving against him, and this will make you bounce up and down instead of moving fluidly.

It may take some experimenting to get the right amount of tension and relaxation in the various parts of your body. A certain amount of tension is needed in the thighs, for instance, to maintain contact with the saddle. Do your gripping to maintain balance with the thighs, as a grip below the knee is a signal to the horse. You should not depend on grip to keep your seat, however. If you relax and learn to move rhythmically with the horse you will begin to develop both a deep seat (glued to the saddle) and the ability to stay on when the horse makes a sudden move.

Problems with the rider's legs are also fairly common. These may be caused by the rider being too stiff, by incorrect stirrup length, or by having the wrong amount of

Many riders lean to one side without realizing it. In this case the rider has dropped her right shoulder as she circles, which makes her whole body twist. "Body English" should not be overdone!

weight in the stirrups. First check your stirrup length and try adjusting them up or down a few notches to see if that helps. You may have to put them in a position that is against the "rules," but remember, you should follow the rules only if they work for you. If changing the stirrups has no effect on your problem, or makes it worse, put them back where they were. Then try relaxing as a solution. Concentrate on relaxing your knees, particularly if you have a tendency to post too high or if you bounce at a trot or jog. If relaxing doesn't work, you probably have either too much weight on your feet or not enough. Try sitting deeper in the saddle and taking weight off your stirrups. Keeping just the toe in the stirrup may cause problems for people with very flexible ankles. With English stirrups the ball of the foot should be resting on the tread of the stirrup. If you have thick, stiff ankles you may be able to put just the toe of the foot on the stirrup and get better results with putting your heels down. Western riders can put the ball of the foot in the stirrup, or put the foot all the way "home," or to the heel. *Caution:* Don't do this unless you have boots with high heels, otherwise your foot may go all the way through the stirrup! Generally, riding with the foot home in the stirrup stiffens the legs too much, but it may work for you.

If you have trouble losing your stirrups and tend to get behind your horse, your stirrups may be too long. Try shortening them a notch or two. If that doesn't help, you may need to put more weight in your stirrups. Do this by sitting more forward in your saddle (not leaning forward but moving forward in the saddle), stretching your legs for the ground and then picking up your stirrups. Then stand in the stirrups and push your heels down as far as they will go. Sit down without letting your heels come back up. This should balance you over your feet. If you then relax your knees, let your weight stay down in the stirrups and keep balanced over your feet so that if the horse disappeared you'd land on your feet; your legs should stay still naturally. Riding an ordinary trot without posting and concentrating on relaxing and letting your hips rock with the horse will also help you to develop a better seat.

Some riders seem to have problems with their hands wandering around where they don't belong. This can also contribute to other riding problems, such as getting left behind when the horse starts up. It is quite common for beginning riders to raise their hands too high while they are concentrating on the rest of their body. It is important for control to keep the hands in front of the body and close to the horse's neck (or fairly close, depending on the horse), and wandering hands can throw the rider off balance as well. I find it helpful for the rider to wind a few strands of the horse's mane around one finger of the rein hand or one hand to hold the hands in the correct position until this becomes a habit.

For the rider who has a problem with his free hand waving around and throwing him off balance or distracting the horse, holding the leg about midway between the knee and hip is helpful. Laying the free hand across the stomach may also work and has the advantage of being near the reins if needed.

A big problem with form that many riders have without realizing it is leaning to one side. Every rider should get a friend to ride behind them to tell them if they have this problem. Most people do it unconsciously because they don't straighten the saddle when they get on and they lean to the left because the saddle was pulled over to the left side of the horse's back when they got on. This puts a strain on the horse's left side, developing it more fully than the right. Many Western riders lean or twist so that

Problems with form are very common, and often interfere with riding fun. This rider seems to be posting with her whole body. This is probably a result of stiff knees and riding on the toes. She should sit down, relax her legs, especially at the knees and ankles, and learn to move with the horse. Even her arms are stiff, which makes her hands go up with the rest of her body. Looking ahead instead of down would help, too. This picture shows a standing martingale in use.

the hand they are riding with pulls that side of their body ahead of the other. If they ride with the right hand this may cause a right-handed horse. This is one reason why I think Western riders should be allowed to shift hands. A rider who rides in a ring often develops a tendency to lean to the inside. This rider usually tilts his whole body, dropping his inside shoulder and often looking down the horse's shoulder instead of straight ahead. This habit may be difficult to overcome if it has been practiced unconsciously for a long time. This is another time when an instructor or observer can be helpful to remind the rider when he is leaning.

Another problem that is very noticeable to an observer and that looks bad is leaning over the horse's shoulder to check a lead, or on a canter depart. This is commonly seen in small horse shows and it is a show judge's pet peeve (at least it's mine). It is easy enough to learn to tell which lead your horse is on without looking for it. One way is to have someone watch you ride and then close your eyes and try to tell which lead the horse is on. You can feel it as one side of the horse (and you) will be slightly ahead of the other. Leaning down to check a lead not only looks ridiculous, but it also puts the horse off balance and may make it difficult to get into a canter properly.

Looking down at your hands or at the horse's shoulder is a bad habit anyway, since it destroys your posture and interferes with your ability to look and think ahead of your horse.

Most riding form problems can be corrected by improving the balance and relaxation of the rider. Once you have mastered the technique of moving with the horse, you will find it easier to give signals with proper timing, and to stay on during the unexpected movements the horse may make such as stumbling, shying, and bucking.

CHAPTER 10

Riding Safety

Riding can be and usually is great fun and good exercise. However, since horses are strong, fast animals and are easily frightened, handling and riding them without observing some safety precautions can be dangerous.

Always remember that horses are timid. They may react violently when startled. A confined or tied horse may kick out if a sudden noise or motion occurs behind him. Always speak to a horse well before you reach him if you are approaching from behind; it is a good idea to speak to him anyway in case he is dozing. This may prevent a tied horse from becoming startled, pulling back, and breaking his tie rope. It is a good idea to tie the horse with a strong rope and halter; never tie him with a bridle. It is quite easy for a horse to break a bridle, and they are expensive to replace. Also, a loose horse with reins dragging may injure his mouth by stepping on the reins and pulling on the bit.

Many riders fall when the horse starts off too soon while they are mounting and off balance. Train your horse to stand until you have settled yourself in the saddle. Don't get into the habit of running up and vaulting on your horse and then kicking him into a trot or canter immediately, or he will start off too soon some day and you will end up dusting your britches off. If you do vault on the horse, teach him to stand and don't let him move off right away. Start the horse out at a walk each time you ride to keep him from wanting to take off just as you mount.

Pick a place to ride that doesn't have hidden obstacles, holes, or soft spots. Avoid riding right next to an old fence that may have loose wires lying in the bushes. If you ride across a field with tall grass or brush, keep to a walk as neither you nor the horse can see holes or stumps. When riding near abandoned houses, watch out for old wells or septic tanks that might cave in. Also avoid clumps of briers or bushes that might have hornets' nests in them.

When you ride with friends, or a friend, be sensible and pay attention to the other horses as well as your own. Don't follow too closely behind another horse no matter how reliable you think he is about not kicking. Any horse will kick if the horse behind him takes a bite out of him, or even just bumps into him. If you ride beside someone, keep a reasonable distance apart so your legs don't get tangled up, so your horses don't fight, and so you don't poke the other horse in the side accidentally with your stirrup. Avoid riding abreast at any gait faster than a walk, except for short distances, as it encourages the horses to race.

If you are at the head of a line of riders or ahead of another horse, give a signal when you are going to speed up or slow down. Make your stops and starts gradual to give the others time to make the transitions without running into you. Don't hold onto low branches and let them swing back behind you, since they will hit the rider behind you in the face. When you have to duck a branch, always lean forward over your horse's neck. Leaning back puts you off balance and if the branch is very low you may be injured if it strikes you in the stomach. When you cross an obstacle such as a creek, wait until everyone in the group has crossed it before speeding up, or their horses will try to start up in the middle of the obstacle. (If anyone has ever done this to you, you'll understand this one!) If someone has to dismount, wait until they have gotten on and are settled before moving off.

If you are riding alone and you come across another rider, call ahead to warn him of your approach, so he can prepare himself in case his horse shies. If you hear someone coming up behind you, turn your horse to face him as soon as you can, so he doesn't shy out from under you.

You can trot or even canter up short hills that aren't too steep, but don't run downhill. It is very difficult for a horse to keep his footing down steep hills, although he may think he wants to run. Also avoid working faster than a trot on wet ground, especially clay or grass, which can be very slippery.

Don't ride a horse double (two people at the same time). This is very hard on the horse's back because it puts the second rider on the weakest part of the back, over his kidneys. Also, most horses will at least try to buck when ridden double, and the second rider may pull the first one off.

Avoid taking a dog or dogs along on your rides, as they will often get into trouble. Also, they may frighten your horse by leaping out of the woods in front of you, and the horse may step on a dog and injure him. The exception to this is the dog that is normally the horse's companion at home anyway and when you are riding in an area away from other houses.

Don't ride with just a halter on your horse. Jumping on the horse in the pasture and letting him take you to the barn is just asking to be bucked off.

Don't clown around or get too relaxed and ride side-saddle on a regular saddle, or in any other position, except in a ring under controlled circumstances. If the horse shies you would undoubtedly fall off, being off balance.

Don't let anyone ride your horse unless you know that he is a competent rider, or is someone you are giving a lesson to. If possible, supervise any riding done by anyone but yourself, so that you don't have to worry about what they did to your horse while you weren't looking.

Always have someone hold a horse that you are getting on for the first time. A strange horse may make a sudden move when you are mounting and you may not be able to stop him.

In short, be alert and think ahead. Most accidents with horses occur because someone was careless and got into a situation they couldn't control.

CHAPTER 11

Lameness and Injuries

Strictly speaking, this chapter doesn't belong in a book on riding, but since some lamenesses and injuries happen while the horse is being ridden I felt they should be discussed.

Hoof care is very important to a riding horse, as poor hoof care often leads to lameness. A horse that is ridden on hard surfaces or rocky ground should probably be shod. Horses with problem feet or minor leg faults such as pigeon toes or splay feet may need corrective shoeing to keep them sound enough to ride.

Care should be taken to keep the horse's hooves trimmed regularly, even if he is not shod, to prevent cracks from forming. As the hoof grows, short cracks may appear at the toe which may stop when pieces of the hoof break off, shortening the toe to the proper length. Unless the horse is ridden a fair amount on hard enough ground to wear the hoof down, however, the rate of growth will exceed the breaking off and the feet will get too long. If the horse's hooves become dry and brittle, the cracks may continue up the hoof and cause lameness. Cracks occurring back toward the heel should be attended to by a blacksmith as soon as they are noticed, as they can cause serious problems. The hooves can be painted with hoof dressing if necessary to keep them from becoming too dry. Ask the blacksmith, not the veterinarian, about hoof care.

Thrush, a fungus infection of the frog, is caused by dirty, wet feet. It is quite common in riding horses, particularly if they are kept in a stall. Thrush can cause lameness if it is allowed to penetrate into the hoof. It can be treated with Clorox bleach or a prepared thrush remedy when it is first noticed. (A foul odor to the hoof is usually the first sign—worse than usual, that is! Later the frog becomes soft and black.) Hold the hoof as you would for cleaning it and pour a little Clorox on it. A severe case of thrush that causes lameness can be treated by the blacksmith by paring the frog away and applying a pack soaked in iodine. (Don't do this yourself!) The daily routine of cleaning the feet and checking for thrush is worth the effort if it prevents thrush from occurring, and it *will* prevent it. Horses that are kept in stalls a lot are prone to thrush. Carefully check a horse you are considering purchasing for thrush.

One of the most common causes of lameness in riding horses is stone bruises. While the wall of the hoof is insensitive, the sole (bottom of the foot) can become bruised and tender if the horse steps on a hard or sharp object. The feet may also become sore if they wear down far enough so that the sole hits the ground when the horse walks. Some horses with poor feet must be kept shod to keep this from happening.

A stone bruise is usually easy to detect as the horse will become suddenly lame while being ridden, usually on gravel. He will noticeably favor one foot and will bob his head. Even a shod horse can get a stone bruise, especially if a rock gets wedged between the shoe and the hoof. If you forgot to clean the horse's feet before you began your ride, a rock imbedded in the dirt in the hoof can cause lameness.

If you are riding along and the horse suddenly begins to limp, get off and check each foot. Tapping the sole of the foot with a rock may help locate the site of the injury. Don't forget to check the heel and coronary band, as a stick may have poked the horse. Feel for a pulse in the heel; it is an indication of fresh injury.

When a horse goes lame while being ridden, you should get off and lead him slowly for a while, after checking his feet. Try to get him onto grass or at least off rocky ground. Feel his legs for heat or swelling in case the problem is a strain or sprain. The horse may stop limping after walking for a while as the pain of the injury subsides. If he stops limping, you can probably get back on, but should walk him home. If he only limped a stride or two, you might be able to continue your ride.

Stone bruises are cured by resting the horse for a few days. Any lameness with no exterior signs of cuts, heat, or swelling can usually be attributed to a bruise, unless you have reason to suspect founder. If the horse seems foot sore in all four feet he may need several weeks of rest for his feet to grow out. If he is like this and is shod, you should probably have the shoes taken off. Horses that get foot sore easily should be shod for riding, however. Horses with very low heels and shallow feet may need special pads to protect their feet.

Horses with poor action, or those who are asked to do quick maneuvers, may interfere with themselves and become injured. The most common interference injuries are caused when the horse either brushes his hoof against the opposite fetlock or overreaches and steps on his heels in front. A horse that interferes badly enough to cut himself or raise bruises should have his feet checked to see if corrective shoeing will help. Have the blacksmith watch him trot and decide what kind of trimming and shoeing will help. (The blacksmith will probably know more about this than the veterinarian.) If the problem cannot be overcome by shoeing or trimming, you may have to get protective boots for the horse. Bell boots, which cover the coronary band and heels of the front feet, protect a horse from overreaching. They can also keep him from landing on his heels when jumping, and can be used as shipping boots, as well. Western horses may need skid boots, which protect the fetlock joints from getting "burned" when sliding to a stop, and are used on the hind legs.

Shin boots may help a horse keep from striking his cannon bones on the inside during spins or other fast work. While boots don't keep a horse from interfering, they do protect him from injury.

When a horse is overworked at strenuous work such as jumping or working in mud, or if he slips or stumbles while traveling at a fast pace, he may suffer a sprain or a pulled tendon. If the horse goes lame and swelling occurs in a joint during or after a ride, it may be a sprain. Depending on the severity of the lameness and swelling, you may want to treat it yourself by applying hot and cold compresses and resting the horse. If you feel it's necessary, you can call the veterinarian, who may give you some more advice, give the horse a shot to make him feel better, and generally ease your mind.

A pulled tendon results in swelling and heat in the tendon area along the cannon bone. If the swelling and heat are mild the injury may be treated with liniment and rest. Severe lameness and swelling should be seen by a veterinarian. Swelling in the tendon area of the hind legs is usually ligament trouble related to the hocks. Swelling of the hocks should be attended to by the veterinarian, who will check for possible spavins. If the horse will not put any weight on a leg, if he points a fore leg, or if he cannot bend a joint, the veterinarian should be called.

Navicular disease can occur in any horse, although it is usually seen in horses with small, narrow feet. It is a degenerative disease of the bone in the hoof that causes great pain and is incurable. It may be brought on or at least aggravated by hard work. Incorrect shoeing and trimming may also precipitate it. Signs of navicular disease are periodic lameness with no apparent cause; pointing one or the other front foot periodically, especially after work; habitual standing with the front feet either camped out in front or back under the horse (positions trying to relieve pain). A horse with diagnosed navicular disease should not be ridden, but if treated with aspirin need not be destroyed. Before considering breeding a horse with navicular disease, the owner should realize that the kind of feet that usually get navicular disease are inherited.

Other injuries that can occur from riding include girth and saddle galls. Girth galls can be treated with a salve. The horse should not be ridden with a saddle until the hair has begun to grow back over the sore, at which time the girth can be used if it is padded. Sometimes a leather girth will cause galls on a thin-skinned horse, in which case a sheepskin pad can be used. Web or string girths seldom cause galls on any horse, unless they are girthed too tight or put on a dirty horse. And of course, a dirty girth can cause sores no matter what it's made of. Sometimes a gall may be rubbed if the saddle is put on too far forward and the girth is too close to the elbow.

Saddle sores on the back, especially near the withers, are often hard to heal. As long as there is tenderness around the spot the horse should not be ridden with a saddle. After the soreness has disappeared the back may be padded carefully and the saddle used, but it should be checked for fit before being used again. Sometimes saddle sores are caused by sloppy saddling, a wrinkle in the blanket, a dirty saddle pad, or inadequate padding. An old saddle may have lumps in the pads that can cause sore spots, and a used saddle should be checked for this. Western saddles should be checked periodically to make sure the "sheepskin" padding underneath has not rubbed away, leaving lumps or rivets exposed. If the horse's withers get rubbed you should either pad your saddle more or shop around and find a saddle with the proper width of tree. You may also be able to get a "cut back" saddle, that has a space cut away at the pommel to accommodate the horse with extra high withers. Any sore on the withers should be considered serious as it may be a beginning fistula, which must be treated by the veterinarian.

Tack

The equipment used with a horse is generally known as "tack." You will need a halter, bridle, saddle, pad, and grooming tools. You could do without a saddle, and ride bareback, and you could dispense with a halter and just use your bridle. You could also ride with a halter and do without a bridle, but most people feel safer and more comfortable with a saddle or at least a bareback pad, and a halter is handy for leading and for tying, as bridles break easily if the horse pulls back when tied.

Some kind of grooming tools are a must. A stiff brush or a rubber curry comb, and something to clean out the hooves (a screwdriver will do) are the absolute minimum needed to keep the horse clean enough so the saddle or girth doesn't rub and to keep the feet clean enough to prevent thrush. Your grooming supplies can also include a soft brush, for brushing away the loose dirt the stiff brush (dandy brush) brings to the surface, a mane comb (an old plastic comb with large teeth does well too), a hoof pick, body rag (for a shine) and a metal curry comb (for cleaning the brushes, not the horse). A shedding blade is useful in the spring to help loosen the winter coat, and a sweat scraper helps speed up drying after a hard workout or a bath. Use of grooming tools is discussed in the chapter on Preparing to Ride.

In the line of tack, you should become familiar with various types of bridles and saddles, and learn their parts (see charts). If you are not going to show your horse, it is not necessary to spend much money on a halter. The inexpensive nylon kind is handy. Nylon has the advantage of being unbreakable, but when you buy a nylon halter, get one with heavy, strong buckles and connecting hardware, as a strong horse may be able to break these if he pulls back when tied. A halter, especially a nylon one, should never be left on a horse when he is turned out, as he will not be able to break it if he gets it caught on something. Also, nylon irritates some horses' skin, causing welts and sore spots. This may make the horse hard to bridle, as the bridle will rub these spots also.

Leather halters are fairly inexpensive (unless you get a fancy show halter). A good leather halter, with stitching instead of rivets, is nearly as strong as nylon, and is easier to keep clean and soft. Riveted halters are weaker than stitched ones, and there is a risk of the horse's breaking any leather halter when tied.

Rope halters are cheaper than either nylon or leather, but are less strong, tend to stretch, and don't look as nice. However, if you are the kind of person who loses things, or if you need to keep a halter on your horse when he's out, a rope halter is handy, as they break easily and are so cheap you can afford to lose them. However, don't try to tie a horse in one, as it is an invitation for him to break away, and you may get him started on a bad habit.

As to size, it is often difficult to judge which size halter you will need. You may end up with several of the wrong size if you aren't careful. Generally, pony halters fit only tiny ponies (under 11 or 12 hands). Colt or foal halters usually fit very young foals (up to two months) or pony foals up to six months if small. Weanling halters fit foals up to about three to four months, except horse foals of some size, which may graduate to yearling size by three months and horse size by a year. A weanling halter may fit a pony that is full grown, however. Yearling colts of horse size may wear a yearling halter if they have a small head, or a cob (small horse) size. The average large pony or small horse (under 15 hands) usually wears a cob size. Those over 15 hands usually wear horse size, although an Arab or Thoroughbred may wear a cob size. There is even a large horse size for 16.2 hands and up.

If you have an old halter, take it and compare sizes, by all means, instead of guessing. You should also measure the horse's head from just above the mouth to just behind the ears and compare this to the length of the halter from top of headstall to the ring on the noseband.

When you buy a halter, you may also buy a lead shank, or you may prefer to make one. Either way, be sure you have one with a strong snap that you can work easily with one hand. This is very important as it is very irritating, and sometimes dangerous, to have to struggle with a stiff or hard to open fastener. The material to use for a lead shank is mainly a matter of preference, although personally I dislike ones with a chain end. While they are useful on hard to manage horses, I find that you usually end up holding the chain part in your hand, which can be painful if the horse jerks away. Avoid materials which will burn your hands if they are pulled through (some kinds of nylon are worse than others), and when you tie the horse with a shank, use one that is at least as strong as the halter, if not stronger. I keep several kinds of lead shanks around—some soft ones for leading, some nylon extra-longs for loading on the trailer, etc. Avoid using baling twine as a lead shank—it's murder on the hands.

If you are going to show your horse, especially in halter (conformation) classes, you will want to get a show halter. If your horse's head is one of his good points, choose an inconspicuous but handsome halter to set his head off; if you want to hide a bad head, especially one with a faulty profile, choose a fancier halter that has tooling, silver or buckstitching to draw the eye away from the contours of the horse's head and to the halter.

If you don't show, you don't necessarily need an English bridle if you ride English style, and vice versa. Many people ride both English and Western, and don't want to buy two bridles, and anyway, Western headstalls are usually less expensive than English ones. Bridles usually come in three sizes—pony, cob and horse. Pony bridles are for small ponies only, remember, and many horses can use a cob size.

As far as bits are concerned, there is truly an amazing array to choose from. Everyone seems to have his favorite, and if you ask for advice on which one to use, you will probably get as many different suggestions as there are bits.

The subject of bitting is a complex one, and it is really impossible to give advice in a book as to which bit is suitable for which horse. However, a knowledge of what kinds of bits there are and how they act on the horse's mouth may help the rider determine which one may fit his particular needs.

Basically, bits fall into two categories: snaffles and curbs. Snaffle bits have rings on the sides but no shanks, and they work on the corners of the horse's mouth. A snaffle is usually found with a jointed mouthpiece, although some have a straight bar or twisted wire mouthpiece. A snaffle does not have a port (hump in the middle of the mouthpiece). The snaffle is a mild bit with no leverage action. The severity of the snaffle depends on the size of the mouthpiece (narrower is harsher) and whether the mouthpiece is twisted (has ridges). A jointed mouthpiece aids in turning with a direct rein, as one side of the bit can work without the other. Because it acts on the corners of the mouth, the snaffle tends to raise the horse's head.

A curb bit is a leverage bit which has shanks on each side. The bit works on the tongue and bars of the mouth (space with no teeth) on each side with leverage created by pulling the reins on the shanks. This causes the mouthpiece to press on the mouth, while the bit turns and puts pressure on the horse's poll by pressing the headstall of the bridle down, and on the chin by pressing the curb strap or chain against it. This three-fold action makes a curb a severe bit.

A curb mouthpiece can be jointed (milder) or ported (the higher the port the more severe). It can have a "cricket," which is a roller in the port for the horse to work his tongue against. A spade bit has a port, a cricket, and a "spoon," which rises up to hit the roof of the mouth when the reins are pulled. The spade is the most severe bit and must be used by only the most skilled of riders.

The shanks of the bit also affect the severity. The longer the shank, the more leverage there is to apply pressure to the mouth, the poll, and the chin. Some curb bits have "loose" shanks that are jointed to the mouthpiece; some are all in one piece.

There are *many* varieties of curbs. They include, in approximate order of severity: the "Tom Thumb," sometimes called a snaffle, sometimes called a Pelham (a combination of snaffle and curb with both snaffle and curb rings for double reins). The Tom Thumb has very short shanks and a jointed mouthpiece and is a very mild curb bit. Most horses work fairly well on this bit and it is a good bit to start with in trying to find a suitable bit for a Western horse. Next in line in severity are the Pelham bits. These are English bits with a straight mouthpiece (usually, although some have jointed mouthpieces or ports). The Pelham also has rings at the mouthpiece for snaffle reins, so the bit can act as either a snaffle or a curb, depending on which set of reins you pull. The Pelham is always used with a curb chain. Shanks range from very short to about eight inches long, and are always straight, whereas curb shanks often curve backward from the mouthpiece.

Next come the many types of plain Western curbs, which usually have a ported mouthpiece. These vary mostly in quality and weight. The cheap, lightweight bits are usually very poor bits which give either very hard or very indefinite action, produce a dry mouth (especially those made of aluminum) and may even bend or break. Choose a bit that is heavy, preferably with a copper mouthpiece, which makes the horse salivate, causing a wet, or "sweet," mouth, aiding sensitivity. A never-rust mouthpiece is a must, and do spend the extra money to get a good bit.

More severe than the run-of-the-mill Western curbs, and used primarily in combination with a small snaffle bit (bridoon) is the English curb (Weymouth). This has long, straight shanks and a fairly thin mouthpiece, usually with a small port. It is used with a curb chain and is very severe. It is also used with the bridoon as a "double" bridle on American Saddle Horses and dressage horses or horses performing advanced English work. It should not be used by the beginning rider. It is comparable to the spade bit in Western riding in that it is very severe and is used by expert riders on highly trained horses.

Mention should also be made of the "quick" bits, which have jointed mouthpieces and loose shanks. These Western bits can be used with double reins and are essentially curb bits. They give excellent results when used properly but can be severe and should be tried only with professional supervision.

The beginning rider should probably start with a plain snaffle bit for English riding and a Tom Thumb for Western riding. He should make sure the bit fits correctly (not pinching the corners of the mouth or sliding back and forth), is adjusted properly (a jointed mouthpiece bit should just pull the corners of the mouth up), and that the noseband is adjusted so the horse cannot open his mouth to evade the bit. The rider should make sure that he is using the reins only to give signals, not to balance himself with, so he is not hanging on the horse's mouth. At the same time, his reins should not be so long that he cannot give signals at the proper time. If the horse keeps throwing his head up out of position (and not because of too strong signals, etc.), a running martingale (adjusted so the rings come up to slightly below the horse's withers in height) may be used to hold his head in position. I do not recommend a standing martingale as it does not correct the horse's head carriage, but only gives him something to brace his neck against. If the horse is just unresponsive to these mild bits (a good sign of this is when he leans into the bit, putting his head down when you pull and lugging forward), then move on to a slightly more severe type. But remember, correct riding techniques can make any horse responsive to mild bits and poor riding can make even a very sensitive horse seem to be unresponsive to severe bits, so make sure you are not causing the problem.

In addition to the many kinds of bits, there are several types of hackamores. A bosal is a rawhide loop that works on the cartilage of the nose, and is used on Western horses, usually only in training. Other hackamores (called mechanical) act on the nose by applying leverage via long shanks and a curb chain. They are like a curb without the mouthpiece. Generally hackamores should be left to trainers and more experienced riders.

When adjusting a bridle, the curb strap or chain should be tight enough to come into play when the reins are pulled, but not so tight that it is in contact when the reins are loose. A too-tight curb strap can cause an otherwise docile horse to rear, back, throw his head, or refuse to stop.

The noseband should be snug, to keep the horse from opening his mouth to avoid the bit. A dropped noseband, which fits below the bit, is used on a horse that has made a habit of dropping his jaw to avoid the bit; a figure eight noseband, which crosses over the horse's face after going under the jaw, does the same thing. These are not allowed in shows.

The throatlatch should be fairly loose. Its purpose is to keep the bridle from slipping over the horse's ears if he should rub on something. Too tight a throatlatch constricts the horse's breathing if he flexes his neck (draws his chin in towards his chest.)

If you use a martingale (called a tie-down Western), adjust it loosely enough to keep it from interfering with the horse's natural balancing gestures (especially when jumping).

Saddles, both English and Western, come in different styles and sizes. Ideally you should fit the saddle to both you and the horse. If you cannot afford to go out and buy just the right saddle for you and the horse, think about him first. You can adjust your riding to fit a saddle that is too big or too small, but an ill-fitting saddle will cause your horse much misery and possibly permanent damage.

Choose a saddle that sits up off the horse's withers even when you are sitting on it. The width of saddles across the back varies greatly, as does the width of horses' backs. If you can buy the saddle with the horse, it may save you a trip to the saddle shop, provided the saddle fits well. It is very difficult to tell whether a saddle really fits or not. Other than seeing that it doesn't press on the withers, you probably can't tell whether it really fits or not. Use at least one good, thick pad, and add extra pads (not more than three at a time) for long rides. Then if your horse gets a sore back even with good padding, a different saddle should be tried.

Western girths (cinches) usually cause no rubbing problems, provided they are not pulled too tight (snug is tight enough) and provided the skin or hair is not pinched in the girth. English leather girths, however, may rub a sensitive horse, especially on a long ride. A sheepskin pad over the girth can be used to prevent this, or you can just use a web or string girth, which seldom causes rubbing. Keeping the girth clean helps prevent rubbing, also.

Saddle pads are important, especially for riders who spend a lot of time in the saddle. Usually it is better to buy real saddle pads or blankets rather than using something from around the house. Towels, old blankets, and scatter rugs are popular substitutes, but usually are either too thin, wrinkle too easily, or chafe. Choose pads that are thick, soft, and that can be washed and dried easily. The exception to this is hair pads, which are very good and must be brushed, not washed. Never use any kind of burlap as a saddle blanket.

In addition to halter, bridle, and saddle, you may find a few other items useful. A long line (15 to 30 feet of rope) can be handy for several things. You can use it for longeing (working the horse in a circle around you for exercise and to teach voice commands), as a back rope when loading on a trailer or when teaching a horse to lead, etc. A longe whip is inexpensive and is a necessity if you are going to longe your horse (I don't longe, I ride them), and a longe whip is handy when loading a recalcitrant horse.

If the saddle slides back on your horse even though it seems to fit all right, a breast strap may be necessary.

If the saddle slides forward all the time, a crupper (which fastens around the tail and to the saddle) may be needed.

If your horse interferes when jumping or doing reining work (cuts himself by striking the lower leg with a hoof), first see your blacksmith; you may need protective boots for him.

And before I forget, a riding crop—preferably a dressage whip, which is longer—is very handy, unless you have a lot of nice young saplings to cut switches from when necessary. Most horses benefit from a sound whack across the rump (never in front of the shoulders, anyway) now and then.

APPENDIX II

Care of Equipment

The worst thing you can do to your tack is to leave it out in the weather. Even if you never really clean it properly, or at least not very often, if you keep your saddle, bridle, etc., in a dry, protected place, they will last practically forever, or at least a lot longer than your horses.

Brushes and grooming tools can be conveniently kept in a bucket, which can be kept in the feed room, tack room (if you have one), or even just in the barn out of the way. Saddles and bridles should be kept out of the weather and where the horse can't reach them, for most horses will chew on leather at least once in a while. Don't hang the saddle pad on the stall, either, or the horse will drag it in and sleep on it. Bridles can be hung on the wall outside the stall, and the saddles can be kept either in a tack box, which is where I keep mine, or put on racks. They can also be left on the floor, in which case you should sit them up on the pommels. If you don't use your saddle nearly every day in the summer, it will get moldy, so check it during periods when you aren't using it to keep the mold from damaging the leather.

Brushes can be cleaned with a metal curry comb, or by rubbing them briskly across the top of a board on a fence or stall. They can also be washed once in a while, but don't overdo it or the bristles fall out. The new nylon bristled brushes are handy in that they clean easily, but I'm not sure how good they are for the horse's coat, so I wouldn't use them every day. Rubber curry combs can be cleaned of caked dirt by banging them on the wall or the heel of your boot.

Clean your halters when they get stiff or mud-encrusted. Nylon and rope halters can be washed, and leather ones get the same treatment as saddles and bridles. (See below.)

Your leather tack (saddles, bridles, martingales, etc.) deserves more careful care if for no other reason than it costs more. Also, it is used so much more that if it is dirty and stiff it may cause discomfort to both the horse and the rider. (Stiff leather reins, for instance, are murder on the hands). Well cared for tack, even is it is cheap, will usually outlast the rider's use of it.

Proper care of bridle and saddle starts with keeping them out of the weather and out of situations which may cause damage. Never tie a horse up with a bridle (use a halter and lead or a rope around the neck). Never turn the horse loose, even in the stall, with the bridle on unless the reins are carefully fastened around the neck so he absolutely can't step on them. (This is practically impossible to do.) When leading the horse with a bridle be sure the reins aren't dragging, as he might step on them. With Western reins, don't leave one rein draped over the horse's neck when leading, as it will amost certainly fall down when your're not looking and get broken. As mentioned before, don't leave tack where the horse can reach it, especially when the horse is tied. It is easy to leave the saddle on the fence next to the horse while you brush him, for instance, but he might pull it off the fence and step on it. Not to mention taking a bite out of the seat in the process. If the tree of the saddle (wooden frame) gets broken, the saddle is ruined, period. Don't let anyone sit on the saddle unless it's on the horse, to keep the tree safe. Don't leave the saddle on the horse at all unless it's tightened up, or it may fall off, or, worse, slip under his belly and cause him to buck and kick. He may catch a foot in it in this case, and tear it to shreds. If you are untacking next to the car, don't put your saddle down on the ground behind it, or even on the back, as you may drive off and forget it, or back over it. (Don't laugh, I did it this year, with my sister's $300 Western saddle!) There are many other dangerous places to put your tack, but these are some examples to get you thinking about how to take care of the couple of hundred dollars' worth of gear you're playing with.

Leather products can be cleaned with several kinds of products. I favor a Lexol type of cleaner which is easier to use than oil and saddle soap. Whatever you use is a matter of preference. Do clean your tack fairly often, though, and at least once a year! I know that sounds silly, but few people actually clean their tack very often, and once a year is about the minimum needed to keep it from actually dry-rotting away. Always let your tack dry thoroughly before cleaning, and if it does get rained on, give it two or three days to dry before oiling it. Don't soak the tack with oil, but apply several coats to get it soft enough.

When you clean your bridle, take it completely apart to do it, or the fasteners will harden up, and eventually the bridle will break where it bends around them. Be careful to study the bridle before you take it apart so you can get it back together right! Make doubly sure the bit is on right and the curb strap is adjusted properly.

English saddles, with their smooth leather, are easy to clean. Western saddles with tooling require a toothbrush to get in the cracks. Give the sheepskin lining on the bottom a good brushing and check it periodically for worn places. Use an extra pad as the padding on the saddle begins to wear thin (which it won't do if you have padded properly in the first place.) If your saddle is getting moldy, try to move it to a dryer place. Don't oil a moldy saddle, as its getting too much moisture already. Do soap it often, though, to protect it. Also, try wrapping it in a clean towel to keep the mold down.

Saddle pads should be hung up somewhere to dry between rides. Don't lay them over the saddle, as this will stain the seat. Don't leave pads lying around on the floor, as the mice will nest in them. This is true of blankets and sheets, too, which should be hung in the stable out of reach of the horses.

Parts of the Tack

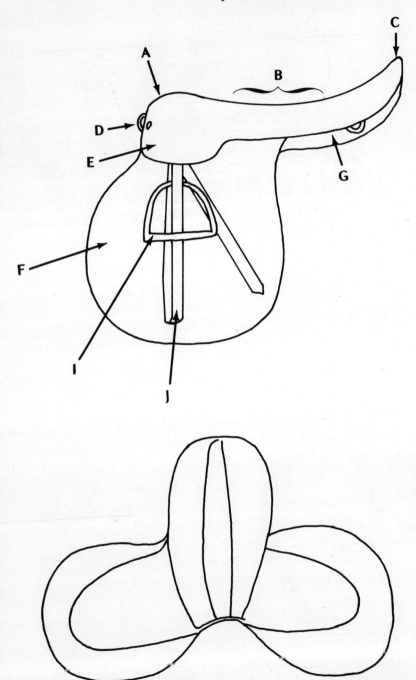

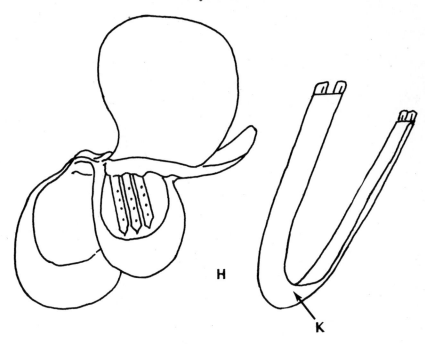

English saddle:

Parts of the saddle:
A. Pommel
B. Seat
C. Cantle
D. Dee ring (to attach breast strap)
    Rear dee ring for hunting attachments such as sandwich case, etc.
E. Jockey
F. Flap
G. Pad
H. Billets (girth fastens here)
I. Stirrup
J. Stirrup leather
K. Girth

Other view shows underneath of saddle.

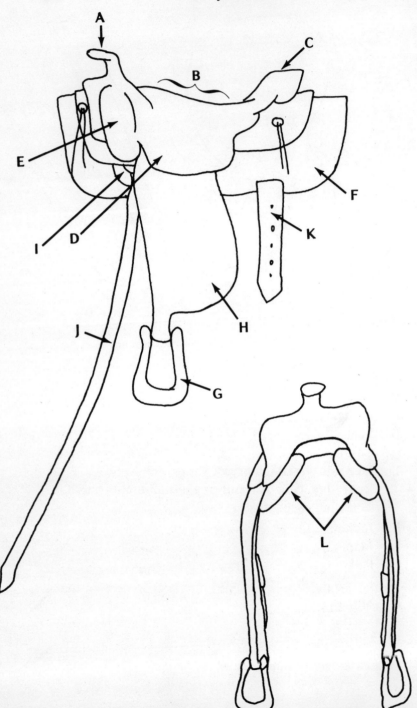

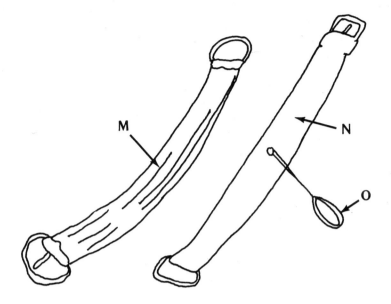

Western Saddle:

A. Horn
B. Seat
C. Cantle
D. Jockey
E. Swell
F. Skirts
G. Stirrup
H. Flap
I. Dee ring for cinch
J. Cinch strap
K. Rear cinch strap
L. Bars of saddle (this is the important part that determines whether or not the saddle is narrow enough to clear the horse's withers but not so narrow that it pinches)
M. Cinch
N. Flank cinch
O. Strap to hook flank cinch to forward cinch

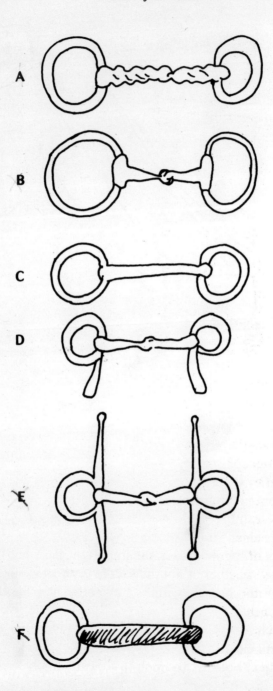

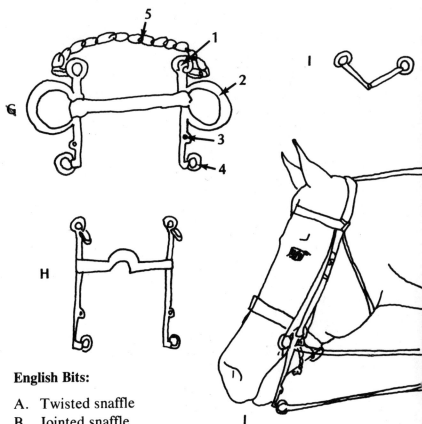

English Bits:

A. Twisted snaffle
B. Jointed snaffle
C. Bar snaffle
D. Half cheek snaffle
E. Fulmer snaffle
F. Rubber mouth snaffle
G. Pelham
    1. headstall hooks to this ring
    2. snaffle rein to this ring
    3. lip strap to this ring (hooks to curb chain)
    4. curb rein to this ring
    5. Curb chain
H. Weymouth, English curb
I. Bridoon
J. A double bridle, showing bridoon and Weymouth
    bits in use

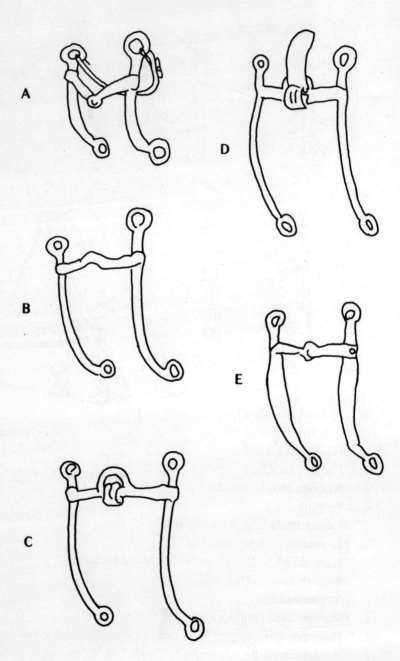

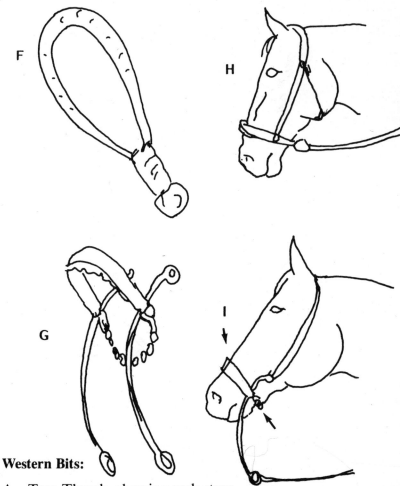

Western Bits:

A. Tom Thumb, showing curb strap
B. Curb bit
C. Half breed bit
D. Spade bit
E. "Quick" bit
F. Bosal
G. Mechanical hackamore (one variety)
H. Showing bosal in use
I. Showing hackamore in use, arrows indicate pressure
   points when reins are pulled

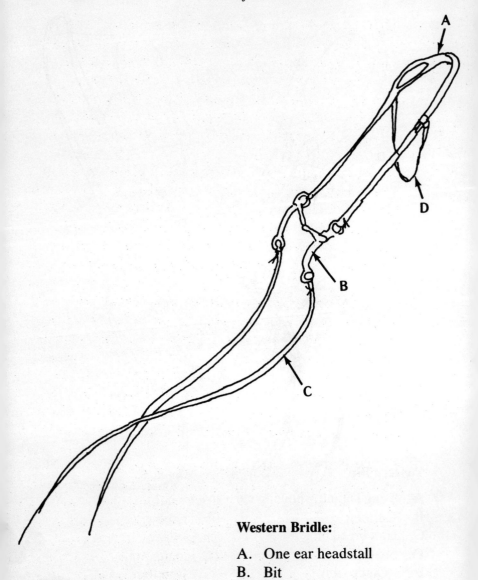

Western Bridle:

A. One ear headstall
B. Bit
C. Reins
D. Throatlatch

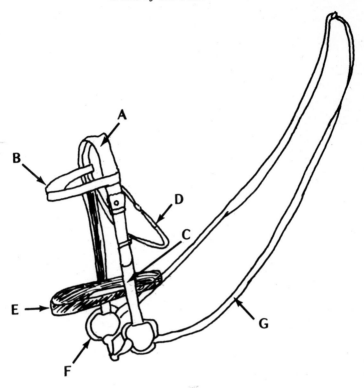

English Bridle:

A. Crownpiece
B. Browband
C. Cheekpiece
D. Throatlatch
E. Cavesson (noseband)
F. Bit
G. Reins

Index

About the Author

Jeanne Posey has been riding since she was seven. She has hunted, shown, trained, and given riding lessons. A former 4-H All Star, she is still active in 4-H programs, having served as an instructor at her district's Horse Science School, coach of the county horse judging team, and chairman of the South Maryland Horse Leaders' Council.

Recently, Mrs. Posey has become interested in long-distance riding, competing in several rides ranging from 20 to 100 miles.

Mrs. Posey is the author of *The Horse Buyer's Guide* and *The Horse Keeper's Guide*. She has a nine-year-old daughter and makes her home in Rison, Maryland.